Measuring

How Long? How Far?

Grade 2

Also appropriate for Grade 1

Anne Goodrow
Douglas H. Clements
Michael T. Battista
Julie Sarama
Joan Akers

Developed at TERC, Cambridge, Massachusetts

Dale Seymour Publications®
White Plains, New York

The *Investigations* curriculum was developed at TERC (formerly
Technical Education Research Centers) in collaboration with Kent State
University and the State University of New York at Buffalo. The work was
supported in part by National Science Foundation Grant No. ESI-9050210.
TERC is a nonprofit company working to improve mathematics and science
education. TERC is located at 2067 Massachusetts Avenue, Cambridge,
MA 02140.

**This project was supported, in part,
by the**
National Science Foundation
Opinions expressed are those of the authors
and not necessarily those of the Foundation

Managing Editor: Catherine Anderson
Grade-Level Editor: Alison Abrohms
Series Editor: Beverly Cory
Revision Team: Laura Marshall Alavosus, Ellen Harding, Patty Green Holubar,
Suzanne Knott, Beverly Hersh Lozoff
ESL Consultant: Nancy Sokol Green
Production/Manufacturing Director: Janet Yearian
Production/Manufacturing Coordinator: Amy Changar, Shannon Miller
Design Manager: Jeff Kelly
Design: Don Taka
Illustrations: Barbara Epstein-Eagle, Laurie Harden, Meryl Treatner
Cover: Bay Graphics
Composition: Archetype Book Composition

This book is published by Dale Seymour Publications®, an imprint of
Addison Wesley Longman, Inc.

Dale Seymour Publications
10 Bank Street
White Plains, NY 10602
Customer Service: 1-800-872-1100

Order number DS43805
ISBN 1-57232-658-1
   4 5 6 7 8 9 10-ML-02 01 00

Printed on Recycled Paper

T E R C

Principal Investigator   Susan Jo Russell

Co-Principal Investigator   Cornelia Tierney

Director of Research and Evaluation   Jan Mokros

Director of K–2 Curriculum   Karen Economopoulos

Curriculum Development
Joan Akers
Michael T. Battista
Mary Berle-Carman
Douglas H. Clements
Karen Economopoulos
Anne Goodrow
Marlene Kliman
Jerrie Moffett
Megan Murray
Ricardo Nemirovsky
Andee Rubin
Susan Jo Russell
Cornelia Tierney
Tracey Wright

Evaluation and Assessment
Mary Berle-Carman
Jan Mokros
Andee Rubin

Teacher Support
Anne Goodrow
Liana Laughlin
Jerrie Moffett
Megan Murray
Tracey Wright

Technology Development
Michael T. Battista
Douglas H. Clements
Julie Sarama

Video Production
David A. Smith
Judy Storeygard

Administration and Production
Irene Baker
Amy Catlin
Amy Taber

**Cooperating Classrooms
for This Unit**
Phyllis Ollove
Boston Public Schools
Boston, MA

Rose Christiansen
Brookline Public Schools
Brookline, MA

Consultants and Advisors
Deborah Lowenberg Ball
Marilyn Burns
Ann Grady
James J. Kaput
Mary M. Lindquist
John Olive
Leslie P. Steffe
Grayson Wheatley

Graduate Assistants
Kathryn Battista
Caroline Borrow
Judy Norris
Kent State University

Julie Sarama
Sudha Swaminathan
Elaine Vukelic
State University of New York at Buffalo

Revisions and Home Materials
Cathy Miles Grant
Marlene Kliman
Margaret McGaffigan
Megan Murray
Kim O'Neil
Andee Rubin
Susan Jo Russell
Lisa Seyferth
Myriam Steinback
Judy Storeygard
Anna Suarez
Cornelia Tierney
Carol Walker
Tracey Wright

CONTENTS

WHERE TO START

The first-time user of *How Long? How Far?* should read the following:

When you next teach this same unit, you can begin to read more of the background. Each time you present the unit, you will learn more about how your students understand the mathematical ideas.

Investigations in Number, Data, and Space® is a K–5 mathematics curriculum with four major goals:

■ to offer students meaningful mathematical problems

■ to emphasize depth in mathematical thinking rather than superficial exposure to a series of fragmented topics

■ to communicate mathematics content and pedagogy to teachers

■ to substantially expand the pool of mathematically literate students

The *Investigations* curriculum embodies a new approach based on years of research about how children learn mathematics. Each grade level consists of a set of separate units, each offering 2–8 weeks of work. These units of study are presented through investigations that involve students in the exploration of major mathematical ideas.

Approaching the mathematics content through investigations helps students develop flexibility and confidence in approaching problems, fluency in using mathematical skills and tools to solve problems, and proficiency in evaluating their solutions. Students also build a repertoire of ways to communicate about their mathematical thinking, while their enjoyment and appreciation of mathematics grows.

The investigations are carefully designed to invite all students into mathematics—girls and boys, members of diverse cultural, ethnic, and language groups, and students with different strengths and interests. Problem contexts often call on students to share experiences from their family, culture, or community. The curriculum eliminates barriers—such as work in isolation from peers, or emphasis on speed and memorization—that exclude some students from participating successfully in mathematics. The following aspects of the curriculum ensure that all students are included in significant mathematics learning:

■ Students spend time exploring problems in depth.

■ They find more than one solution to many of the problems they work on.

■ They invent their own strategies and approaches, rather than rely on memorized procedures.

■ They choose from a variety of concrete materials and appropriate technology, including calculators, as a natural part of their everyday mathematical work.

■ They express their mathematical thinking through drawing, writing, and talking.

■ They work in a variety of groupings—as a whole class, individually, in pairs, and in small groups.

■ They move around the classroom as they explore the mathematics in their environment and talk with their peers.

While reading and other language activities are typically given a great deal of time and emphasis in elementary classrooms, mathematics often does not get the time it needs. If students are to experience mathematics in depth, they must have enough time to become engaged in real mathematical problems. We believe that a minimum of 5 hours of mathematics classroom time a week—about an hour a day—is critical at the elementary level. The scope and pacing of the *Investigations* curriculum are based on that belief.

We explain more about the pedagogy and principles that underlie these investigations in Teacher Notes throughout the units. For correlations of the curriculum to the NCTM Standards and further help in using this research-based program for teaching mathematics, see the following books, available from Dale Seymour Publications:

■ *Implementing the* Investigations in Number, Data, and Space® *Curriculum*

■ *Beyond Arithmetic: Changing Mathematics in the Elementary Classroom* by Jan Mokros, Susan Jo Russell, and Karen Economopoulos

This book is one of the curriculum units for *Investigations in Number, Data, and Space.* In addition to providing part of a complete mathematics curriculum for your students, this unit offers information to support your own professional development. You, the teacher, are the person who will make this curriculum come alive in the classroom; the book for each unit is your main support system.

Although the curriculum does not include student textbooks, reproducible sheets for student work are provided in the unit and are also available as Student Activity Booklets. Students work actively with objects and experiences in their own environment and with a variety of manipulative materials and technology, rather than with a book of instruction and problems. We strongly recommend use of the overhead projector as a way to present problems, to focus group discussion, and to help students share ideas and strategies.

Ultimately, every teacher will use these investigations in ways that make sense for his or her particular style, the particular group of students, and the constraints and supports of a particular school environment. Each unit offers information and guidance for a wide variety of situations, drawn from our collaborations with many teachers and students over many years. Our goal in this book is to help you, a professional educator, implement this curriculum in a way that will give all your students access to mathematical power.

Investigation Format

The opening two pages of each investigation help you get ready for the work that follows.

What Happens This gives a synopsis of each session or block of sessions.

Mathematical Emphasis This lists the most important ideas and processes students will encounter in this investigation.

What to Plan Ahead of Time These lists alert you to materials to gather, sheets to duplicate, transparencies to make, and anything else you need to do before starting.

INVESTIGATION 1

Comparing Lengths

What Happens

Session 1: Scavenger Hunt Students find items that are *about* the same length as each of several strips of adding machine tape that are posted around the room. They compare the length of the items with the length of the strips, and for each length, record the items they find that match.

Sessions 2, 3, and 4: A Scavenger Hunt Choice Time Students work on three activities in Choice Time over the three sessions. They use nonstandard units to find things that are a certain number of units long, then predict and measure how long those items are when a related nonstandard unit is used. This activity is used as a Teacher Checkpoint. Students are also introduced to Steps, a computer activity in which the *Geo-Logo* turtle is moved by unit lengths.

Sessions 5, 6, and 7: Choices About Measurement Students are introduced to three additional choices. In How Far Can You Jump? and Measurement Riddles they measure and compare lengths. In Giant Steps, a computer activity, they move a "turtle" by different-sized unit lengths. Scavenger Hunt 2: How Many Paper Strips?, is another choice for these sessions. A class discussion at the end of Session 7 gives students the opportunity to talk about and reflect on their work.

Session 8: Measuring Our Classroom As an assessment, students use units of their own choosing to measure the width of the classroom. As a class, they discuss the variety of measures they found.

Mathematical Emphasis

■ Using direct and indirect comparison to compare lengths
■ Using a nonstandard unit to measure length
■ Comparing the effects of measurement using units of different size
■ Communicating the need for using a standard unit

INVESTIGATION 1

What to Plan Ahead of Time

Materials

■ Materials that can be used as nonstandard units of measure, such as craft sticks, paper clips, straws: enough to measure the length or width of your classroom (all sessions)
■ Interlocking cubes: about 30 per student (all sessions)
■ String or ribbon: 2–3 rolls. Yarn is not recommended because it stretches easily. (Sessions 1–4)
■ Student math folders: 1 per student (Session 1)
■ Adding machine tape: 3–6 rolls (all sessions)
■ Chart paper (Sessions 1–5, 8)
■ 6″ blue paper strips cut from blue index cards or construction paper: 5 per student (Sessions 2–8)
■ 3″ yellow paper strips cut from yellow index cards or construction paper: 10 per student (Sessions 2–8)
■ Game or place markers such as cubes, pennies, and paper clips (Sessions 5–7)
■ Computers: Macintosh II or above, with 4 MB of internal memory (RAM) and Apple System Software 7.0 or later: 1 per 4–6 students (Sessions 2–7)
■ A projection device or large-screen monitor on one computer for whole-class viewing (Sessions 2–7, optional)
■ Apple Macintosh disk, *Geo-Logo* (Sessions 2–7)
■ Masking tape (Sessions 2–7)
■ Scissors (Session 5)

Other Preparation

■ Duplicate student sheets and teaching resources (located at the end of this unit) in the following quantities. If you have Student Activity Booklets, copy only the items marked with an asterisk.

For Session 1
Student Sheet 1, Weekly Log (p. 135): 1 per student. At this time, you may wish to duplicate a supply to last for the entire unit and distribute the sheets as needed.
Student Sheets 2 and 3, Scavenger Hunt 1 (pp. 136–137): 1 each per student
Student Sheet 4, Finding Similar Lengths (p. 138): 1 per student (homework)
Family letter* (p. 134): 1 per student. Remember to sign and date the letter before copying it.

For Sessions 2–4
Student Sheet 5, Scavenger Hunt 2 (p. 139): 1 per student (class), 1 per student (homework)
Geo-Logo User Sheet* (p. 161): Post one copy beside each computer.
Student Sheet 6, Scavenger Hunt 2 (p. 140): 1 per student
Student Sheet 7, Measuring Strips (p. 141): 1 per student (homework), plus extras*

For Sessions 5–7
Student Sheet 8, How Far Can You Jump? (p. 142): 1 per student

Continued on next page

Sessions Within an investigation, the activities are organized by class session, a session being at least a one-hour math class. Sessions are numbered consecutively through an investigation. Often several sessions are grouped together, presenting a block of activities with a single major focus.

When you find a block of sessions presented together—for example, Sessions 1, 2, and 3—read through the entire block first to understand the overall flow and sequence of the activities. Make some preliminary decisions about how you will divide the activities into three sessions for your class, based on what you know about your students. You may need to modify your initial plans as you progress through the activities, and you may want to make notes in the margins of the pages as reminders for the next time you use the unit.

Be sure to read the Session Follow-Up section at the end of the session block to see what homework assignments and extensions are suggested as you make your initial plans.

While you may be used to a curriculum that tells you exactly what each class session should cover, we have found that the teacher is in a better position to make these decisions. Each unit is flexible and may be handled somewhat differently by every teacher. Although we provide guidance for how many sessions a particular group of activities is likely to need, we want you to be active in determining an appropriate pace and the best transition points for your class. It is not unusual for a teacher to spend more or less time than is proposed for the activities.

Classroom Routines The Start-Up at the beginning of each session offers suggestions for how to acknowledge and integrate homework from the previous session, and which Classroom Routine activities to include sometime during the school day. Routines provide students with regular practice in important mathematical skills such as solving number combinations, collecting and organizing data, understanding time, and seeing spatial relationships. Two routines, How Many Pockets? and Today's Number, are used regularly in the grade 2 *Investigations* units. A third routine, Time and Time Again, appears in the final unit, *Timelines and Rhythm Patterns*. This routine provides a variety of activities about understanding

---

Session 8

Measuring Our Classroom

What Happens

As an assessment, students use units of their own choosing to measure the width of the classroom. As a class, they discuss the variety of measures they found. Their work focuses on:

■ iterating units

■ thinking about the need for a standard unit

Start-Up

Today's Number

Calendar Date *and* **Number of School Days** Students can express today's number using coins (pennies, nickels, dimes, quarters). For example, if the number is 28 (calendar date) possible combinations are: 25¢ + 1¢ + 1¢ + 1¢ or 10¢ + 10¢ + 5¢ + 1¢ + 1¢ + 1¢. If Today's Number is over 100, such as 137, a possible combination is 25¢ + 25¢ + 25¢ + 25¢ + 10¢ + 1¢ + 1¢. If you are counting the number of school days, add a card to the class counting strip and fill in another number on the blank 200 chart.

Materials

■ Interlocking cubes (about 30 per student)

■ Blue and yellow paper strips (from Sessions 2, 3, and 4)

■ Other nonstandard measuring units such as craft sticks

■ Chart paper

Activity

Assessment

Measuring Our Classroom

Choose one dimension of your classroom (length or width) for students to measure. Since students may choose small units of measure and require a large number of units, you may want to have them measure the smaller dimension of the room.

Because the terms *how wide* or *width* may not be familiar to some students, point out the width of the classroom as you introduce this activity.

Since we have been working with measuring, I've been wondering about how wide our classroom is. Can you think of a reason why we might need to know the width of our classroom?

Today, you'll be working with partners to measure the width of the classroom. You and your partner will need to agree on what you will use to measure with. You can use the blue paper strips or the yellow paper strips. Or you might want to use cubes, or paper clips, or craft sticks [*or other nonstandard units*]. You will also need to decide *how* you will use your tools to figure out how wide our classroom is.

---

time; these can be easily integrated throughout the school day and into other parts of the classroom curriculum. A fourth routine, Quick Images, supports work in the unit *Shapes, Halves, and Symmetry*. After its introduction, you might do it once or twice a week to develop students' visual sense of number (as displayed in dot arrangements).

Most Classroom Routine activities are short and can be done whenever you have a spare 10 minutes—maybe before lunch or recess, or at the beginning or end of the day. Complete descriptions of the Classroom Routines can be found at the end of the units.

Activities The activities include pair and small-group work, individual tasks, and whole-class discussions. In any case, students are seated together, talking and sharing ideas during all work times. Students most often work cooperatively, although each student may record work individually.

Choice Time In most units, some sessions are structured with activity choices. In these cases, students may work simultaneously on different activities focused on the same mathematical ideas.

Students choose which activities they want to do, and they cycle through them.

You will need to decide how to set up and introduce these activities and how to let students make their choices. Some teachers set up choices as stations around the room, while others post the list of available choices and allow students to collect their own materials and choose their own work space. You may need to experiment with a few different structures before finding a set up that works best for you, your students, and your classroom.

Tips for the Linguistically Diverse Classroom At strategic points in each unit, you will find concrete suggestions for simple modifications of the teaching strategies to encourage the participation of all students. Many of these tips offer alternative ways to elicit critical thinking from students at varying levels of English proficiency, as well as from other students who find it difficult to verbalize their thinking.

The tips are supported by suggestions for specific vocabulary work to help ensure that all students can participate fully in the investigations. The Preview for the Linguistically Diverse Classroom lists important words that are assumed as part of the working vocabulary of the unit. Second-language learners will need to become familiar with these words in order to understand the problems and activities they will be doing. These terms can be incorporated into students' second-language work before or during the unit. Activities that can be used to present the words are found in the appendix, Vocabulary Support for Second-Language Learners. In addition, ideas for making connections to students' languages and cultures, included on the Preview page, help the class explore the unit's concepts from a multicultural perspective.

Session Follow-Up: Homework In *Investigations,* homework is an extension of classroom work. Sometimes it offers review and practice of work done in class, sometimes preparation for upcoming activities, and sometimes numerical practice that revisits work in earlier units. Homework plays a role both in supporting students' learning and in helping inform families about the ways in which students in this curriculum work with mathematical ideas.

Depending on your school's homework policies and your own judgment, you may want to assign more homework than is suggested in the units. For this purpose you might use the practice pages, included as blackline masters at the end of this unit, to give students additional work with numbers.

For some homework assignments, you will want to adapt the activity to meet the needs of a variety of students in your class: those with special needs, those ready for more challenge, and second-language learners. You might change the numbers in a problem, make the activity more or less complex, or go through a sample activity with those who need extra help. You can modify any student sheet for either homework or class use. In particular, making numbers in a problem smaller or larger can make the same basic activity appropriate for a wider range of students.

Another issue to consider is how to handle the homework that students bring back to class—how to recognize the work they have done at home without spending too much time on it. Some teachers hold a short group discussion of different approaches to the assignment; others ask students to share and discuss their work with a neighbor; still others post the homework around the room

and give students time to tour it briefly. If you want to keep track of homework students bring in, be sure it ends up in a designated place.

Session Follow-Up: Extensions Sometimes in Session Follow-Up, you will find suggested extension activities. These are opportunities for some or all students to explore a topic in greater depth or in a different context. They are not designed for "fast" students; mathematics is a multifaceted discipline, and different students will want to go further in different investigations. Look for and encourage the sparks of interest and enthusiasm you see in your students, and use the extensions to help them pursue these interests.

Excursions Some of the *Investigations* units include excursions—blocks of activities that could be omitted without harming the integrity of the unit. This is one way of dealing with the great depth and variety of elementary mathematics— much more than a class has time to explore in any one year. Excursions give you the flexibility to make different choices from year to year, doing the excursion in one unit this time, and next year trying another excursion.

Materials

A complete list of the materials needed for teaching this unit follows the unit overview. Some of these materials are available in kits for the *Investigations* curriculum. Individual items can also be purchased from school supply dealers.

Classroom Materials In an active mathematics classroom, certain basic materials should be available at all times: interlocking cubes, pencils, unlined paper, graph paper, calculators, and things to count with. Some activities in this curriculum require scissors and glue sticks or tape. Stick-on notes and large paper are also useful materials throughout.

So that students can independently get what they need at any time, they should know where these materials are kept, how they are stored, and how they are to be returned to the storage area. Many teachers have found that stopping 5 minutes before the end of each session so that students can finish their work and clean up is helpful in maintaining classroom materials. You'll find that establishing such routines at the beginning of the year is well worth the time and effort.

Student Sheets and Teaching Resources Student recording sheets and other teaching tools needed for both class and homework are provided as reproducible blackline masters at the end of each unit.

We think it's important that students find their own ways of organizing and recording their work. They need to learn how to explain their thinking with both drawings and written words, and how to organize their results so someone else can understand them. For this reason, we deliberately do not provide student sheets for every activity. Regardless of the form in which students do their work, we recommend that they keep their work in a mathematics folder, notebook, or journal so that it is always available to them for reference.

Student Activity Booklets These booklets contain all the sheets each student will need for individual work, freeing you from extensive copying (although you may need or want to copy the occasional teaching resource on transparency film or card stock, or make extra copies of a student sheet).

Calculators and Computers Calculators are introduced to students in the second unit of the grade 2 sequence, *Coins, Coupons, and Combinations*. It is assumed that calculators are readily available throughout the curriculum.

Computer activities are offered at all grade levels. Although the software is linked to activities in three units in grade 2, we recommend that students use it throughout the year. As students use the software over time, they continue to develop skills presented in the units. How you incorporate the computer activities into your curriculum depends on the number of computers you have available. Technology in the Curriculum discusses ways to incorporate the use of calculators and computers into classroom activities.

Children's Literature Each unit offers a list of related children's literature that can be used to support the mathematical ideas in the unit. Sometimes an activity is based on a selected children's book, with suggestions for substitutions where practical. While such activities can be adapted and taught without the book, the literature offers a rich introduction and should be used whenever possible.

Investigations at Home It is a good idea to make your policy on homework explicit to both students and their families when you begin teaching with *Investigations*. How frequently will you be assigning homework? When do you expect homework to be completed and brought back to school? What are your goals in assigning homework? How independent should families expect their children to be? What should the parent's or guardian's role be? The more explicit you can be about your expectations, the better the homework experience will be for everyone.

Investigations at Home (a booklet available separately for each unit, to send home with students) gives you a way to communicate with families about the work students are doing in class. This booklet includes a brief description of every session, a list of the mathematics content emphasized in each investigation, and a discussion of each homework assignment to help families more effectively support their children. Whether or not you are using the *Investigations* at Home booklets, we

expect you to make your own choices about homework assignments. Feel free to omit any and to add extra ones you think are appropriate.

Family Letter A letter that you can send home to students' families is included with the blackline masters for each unit. Families need to be informed about the mathematics work in your classroom; they should be encouraged to participate in and support their children's work. A reminder to send home the letter for each unit appears in one of the early investigations. These letters are also available separately in Spanish, Vietnamese, Cantonese, Hmong, and Cambodian.

Help for You, the Teacher

Because we believe strongly that a new curriculum must help teachers think in new ways about mathematics and about their students' mathematical thinking processes, we have included a great deal of material to help you learn more about both.

About the Mathematics in This Unit This introductory section summarizes the critical informa-

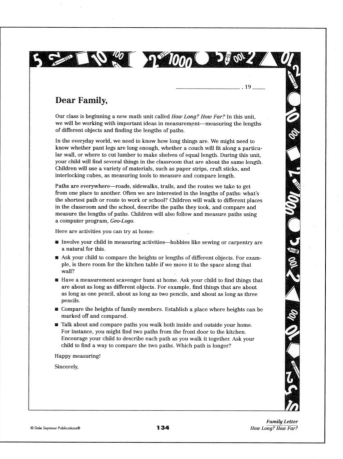

134

Family Letter
How Long? How Far?

tion about the mathematics you will be teaching. It describes the unit's central mathematical ideas and the ways students will encounter them through the unit's activities.

About the Assessment in This Unit This introductory section highlights Teacher Checkpoints and assessment activities contained in the unit. It offers questions to stimulate your assessment as you observe the development of students' mathematical thinking and learning.

Teacher Notes These reference notes provide practical information about the mathematics you are teaching and about our experience with how students learn. Many of the notes were written in response to actual questions from teachers or to discuss important things we saw happening in the field-test classrooms. Some teachers like to read them all before starting the unit, then review them as they come up in particular investigations.

Dialogue Boxes Sample dialogues demonstrate how students typically express their mathematical ideas, what issues and confusions arise in their thinking, and how some teachers have guided class discussions.

These dialogues are based on the extensive classroom testing of this curriculum; many are word-for-word transcriptions of recorded class discussions. They are not always easy reading; sometimes it may take some effort to unravel what the students are trying to say. But this is the value of these dialogues; they offer good clues to how your students may develop and express their approaches and strategies, helping you prepare for your own class discussions.

Where to Start You may not have time to read everything the first time you use this unit. As a first-time user, you will likely focus on understanding the activities and working them out with your students. Read completely through all the activities before starting to present them. Also read those sections listed in the Contents under the heading Where to Start.

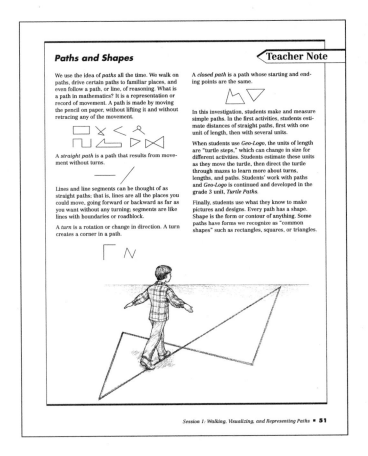

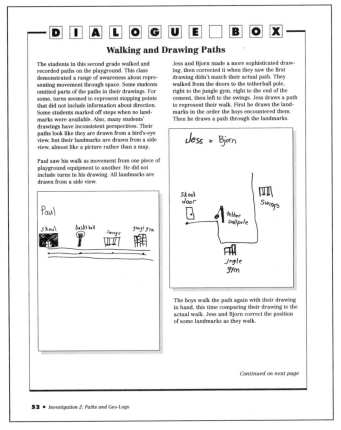

The *Investigations* curriculum incorporates the use of two forms of technology in the classroom: calculators and computers. Calculators are assumed to be standard classroom materials, available for student use in any unit. Computers are explicitly linked to one or more units at each grade level; they are used with the unit on 2-D geometry at each grade, as well as with some of the units on measuring, data, and changes.

Using Calculators

In this curriculum, calculators are considered tools for doing mathematics, similar to pattern blocks or interlocking cubes. Just as with other tools, students must learn both *how* to use calculators correctly and *when* they are appropriate to use. This knowledge is crucial for daily life, as calculators are now a standard way of handling numerical operations, both at work and at home.

Using a calculator correctly is not a simple task; it depends on a good knowledge of the four operations and of the number system, so that students can select suitable calculations and also determine what a reasonable result would be. These skills are the basis of any work with numbers, whether or not a calculator is involved.

Unfortunately, calculators are often seen as tools to check computations with, as if other methods are somehow more fallible. Students need to understand that any computational method can be used to check any other; it's just as easy to make a mistake on the calculator as it is to make a mistake on paper or with mental arithmetic. Throughout this curriculum, we encourage students to solve computation problems in more than one way in order to double-check their accuracy. We present mental arithmetic, paper-and-pencil computation, and calculators as three possible approaches.

In this curriculum we also recognize that, despite their importance, calculators are not always appropriate in mathematics instruction. Like any tools, calculators are useful for some tasks but not for others. You will need to make decisions about when to allow students access to calculators and when to ask that they solve problems without

them so that they can concentrate on other tools and skills. At times when calculators are or are not appropriate for a particular activity, we make specific recommendations. Help your students develop their own sense of which problems they can tackle with their own reasoning and which ones might be better solved with a combination of their own reasoning and the calculator.

Managing calculators in your classroom so that they are a tool, and not a distraction, requires some planning. When calculators are first introduced, students often want to use them for everything, even problems that can be solved quite simply by other methods. However, once the novelty wears off, students are just as interested in developing their own strategies, especially when these strategies are emphasized and valued in the classroom. Over time, students will come to recognize the ease and value of solving problems mentally, with paper and pencil, or with manipulatives, while also understanding the power of the calculator to facilitate work with larger numbers.

Experience shows that if calculators are available only occasionally, students become excited and distracted when they are permitted to use them. They focus on the tool rather than on the mathematics. In order to learn when calculators are appropriate and when they are not, students must have easy access to them and use them routinely in their work.

If you have a calculator for each student, and if you think your students can accept the responsibility, you might allow them to keep their calculators with the rest of their individual materials, at least for the first few weeks of school. Alternatively, you might store them in boxes on a shelf, number each calculator, and assign a corresponding number to each student. This system can give students a sense of ownership while also helping you keep track of the calculators.

Using Computers

Students can use computers to approach and visualize mathematical situations in new ways. The computer allows students to construct and manipulate geometric shapes, see objects move according to rules they specify, and turn, flip, and repeat a pattern.

This curriculum calls for computers in units where they are a particularly effective tool for learning mathematics content. One unit on 2-D geometry at each of the grades 3–5 includes a core of activities that rely on access to computers, either in the classroom or in a lab. Other units on geometry, measuring, data, and changes include computer activities, but can be taught without them. In these units, however, students' experience is greatly enhanced by computer use.

The following list outlines the recommended use of computers in this curriculum:

Kindergarten
Unit: *Making Shapes and Building Blocks* (Exploring Geometry)
Software: *Shapes*
Source: provided with the unit

Grade 1
Unit: *Survey Questions and Secret Rules* (Collecting and Sorting Data)
Software: *Tabletop, Jr.*
Source: Broderbund

Unit: *Quilt Squares and Block Towns* (2-D and 3-D Geometry)
Software: *Shapes*
Source: provided with the unit

Grade 2
Unit: *Mathematical Thinking at Grade 2* (Introduction)
Software: *Shapes*
Source: provided with the unit

Unit: *Shapes, Halves, and Symmetry* (Geometry and Fractions)
Software: *Shapes*
Source: provided with the unit

Unit: *How Long? How Far?* (Measuring)
Software: *Geo-Logo*
Source: provided with the unit

Grade 3
Unit: *Flips, Turns, and Area* (2-D Geometry)
Software: *Tumbling Tetrominoes*
Source: provided with the unit

Unit: *Turtle Paths* (2-D Geometry)
Software: *Geo-Logo*
Source: provided with the unit

Grade 4
Unit: *Sunken Ships and Grid Patterns* (2-D Geometry)
Software: *Geo-Logo*
Source: provided with the unit

Grade 5
Unit: *Picturing Polygons* (2-D Geometry)
Software: *Geo-Logo*
Source: provided with the unit

Unit: *Patterns of Change* (Tables and Graphs)
Software: *Trips*
Source: provided with the unit

Unit: *Data: Kids, Cats, and Ads* (Statistics)
Software: *Tabletop, Sr.*
Source: Broderbund

The software provided with the *Investigations* units uses the power of the computer to help students explore mathematical ideas and relationships that cannot be explored in the same way with physical materials. With the *Shapes* (grades 1–2) and *Tumbling Tetrominoes* (grade 3) software, students explore symmetry, pattern, rotation and reflection, area, and characteristics of 2-D shapes. With the *Geo-Logo* software (grades 2–5), students investigate rotations and reflections, coordinate geometry, the properties of 2-D shapes, and angles. The *Trips* software (grade 5) is a mathematical exploration of motion in which students run experiments and interpret data presented in graphs and tables.

We suggest that students work in pairs on the computer; this not only maximizes computer resources but also encourages students to consult, monitor, and teach each other. Generally, more than two students at one computer find it difficult to share. Managing access to computers is an issue for every classroom. The curriculum gives you explicit support for setting up a system. The units are structured on the assumption that you have enough computers for half your students to work on the machines in pairs at one time. If you do not have access to that many computers, suggestions are made for structuring class time to use the unit with fewer than five.

Assessment plays a critical role in teaching and learning, and it is an integral part of the *Investigations* curriculum. For a teacher using these units, assessment is an ongoing process. You observe students' discussions and explanations of their strategies on a daily basis and examine their work as it evolves. While students are busy recording and representing their work, working on projects, sharing with partners, and playing mathematical games, you have many opportunities to observe their mathematical thinking. What you learn through observation guides your decisions about how to proceed. In any of the units, you will repeatedly consider questions like these:

- Do students come up with their own strategies for solving problems, or do they expect others to tell them what to do? What do their strategies reveal about their mathematical understanding?

- Do students understand that there are different strategies for solving problems? Do they articulate their strategies and try to understand other students' strategies?

- How effectively do students use materials as tools to help with their mathematical work?

- Do students have effective ideas for keeping track of and recording their work? Do keeping track of and recording their work seem difficult for them?

You will need to develop a comfortable and efficient system for recording and keeping track of your observations. Some teachers keep a clipboard handy and jot notes on a class list or on adhesive labels that are later transferred to student files. Others keep loose-leaf notebooks with a page for each student and make weekly notes about what they have observed in class.

Assessment Tools in the Unit

With the activities in each unit, you will find questions to guide your thinking while observing the students at work. You will also find two built-in assessment tools: Teacher Checkpoints and embedded Assessment activities.

Teacher Checkpoints The designated Teacher Checkpoints in each unit offer a time to "check in" with individual students, watch them at work, and ask questions that illuminate how they are thinking.

At first it may be hard to know what to look for, hard to know what kinds of questions to ask. Students may be reluctant to talk; they may not be accustomed to having the teacher ask them about their work, or they may not know how to explain their thinking. Two important ingredients of this process are asking students open-ended questions about their work and showing genuine interest in how they are approaching the task. When students see that you are interested in their thinking and are counting on them to come up with their own ways of solving problems, they may surprise you with the depth of their understanding.

Teacher Checkpoints also give you the chance to pause in the teaching sequence and reflect on how your class is doing overall. Think about whether you need to adjust your pacing: Are most students fluent with strategies for solving a particular kind of problem? Are they just starting to formulate good strategies? Or are they still struggling with how to start? Depending on what you see as the students work, you may want to spend more time on similar problems, change some of the problems to use smaller numbers, move quickly to more challenging material, modify subsequent activities for some students, work on particular ideas with a small group, or pair students who have good strategies with those who are having more difficulty.

Embedded Assessment Activities Assessment activities embedded in each unit will help you examine specific pieces of student work, figure out what they mean, and provide feedback. From the students' point of view, these assessment activities are no different from any others. Each is a learning experience in and of itself, as well as an opportunity for you to gather evidence about students' mathematical understanding.

The embedded assessment activities sometimes involve writing and reflecting; at other times, a discussion or brief interaction between student and teacher; and in still other instances, the creation and explanation of a product. In most cases, the assessments require that students *show* what they did, *write* or *talk* about it, or do both. Having to explain how they worked through a problem helps students be more focused and clear in their mathematical thinking. It also helps them realize that doing mathematics is a process that may involve tentative starts, revising one's approach, taking different paths, and working through ideas.

Teachers often find the hardest part of assessment to be interpreting their students' work. We provide guidelines to help with that interpretation. If you have used a process approach to teaching writing, the assessment in *Investigations* will seem familiar. For many of the assessment activities, a Teacher Note provides examples of student work and a commentary on what it indicates about student thinking.

Documentation of Student Growth

To form an overall picture of mathematical progress, it is important to document each student's work. Many teachers have students keep their work in folders, notebooks, or journals, and some like to have students summarize their learning in journals at the end of each unit. It's important to document students' progress, and we recommend that you keep a portfolio of selected work for each student, unit by unit, for the entire year. The final activity in each *Investigations* unit, called Choosing Student Work to Save, helps you and the students select representative samples for a record of their work.

This kind of regular documentation helps you synthesize information about each student as a mathematical learner. From different pieces of evidence, you can put together the big picture. This synthesis will be invaluable in thinking about where to go next with a particular child, deciding where more work is needed, or explaining to parents (or other teachers) how a child is doing.

If you use portfolios, you need to collect a good balance of work, yet avoid being swamped with an overwhelming amount of paper. Following are some tips for effective portfolios:

- Collect a representative sample of work, including some pieces that students themselves select for inclusion in the portfolio. There should be just a few pieces for each unit, showing different kinds of work—some assignments that involve writing as well as some that do not.

- If students do not date their work, do so yourself so that you can reconstruct the order in which pieces were done.

- Include your reflections on the work. When you are looking back over the whole year, such comments are reminders of what seemed especially interesting about a particular piece; they can also be helpful to other teachers and to parents. Older students should be encouraged to write their own reflections about their work.

Assessment Overview

There are two places to turn for a preview of the assessment opportunities in each *Investigations* unit. The Assessment Resources column in the unit Overview Chart identifies the Teacher Checkpoints and Assessment activities embedded in each investigation, guidelines for observing the students that appear within classroom activities, and any Teacher Notes and Dialogue Boxes that explain what to look for and what types of student responses you might expect to see in your classroom. Additionally, the section About the Assessment in This Unit gives you a detailed list of questions for each investigation, keyed to the mathematical emphases, to help you observe student growth.

Depending on your situation, you may want to provide additional assessment opportunities. Most of the investigations lend themselves to more-frequent assessment, simply by having students do more writing and recording while they are working.

How Long? How Far?

Content of This Unit Students explore <u>linear measurement</u> by finding and comparing lengths and using nonstandard units to measure length. In the first investigation, students use nonstandard units to measure length. They develop strategies for iterating and counting units, and explore the relationship between size and the number of units needed. In the second investigation, students construct and measure simple paths, estimate the length of paths, and investigate turns in both on- and off-computer activities.

This unit, in particular Investigation 2, uses computers. Although this unit can be done without computers, computer activities are motivating and engage students in using measurement as they construct paths and geometric shapes on the computer.

Ways You Might Use This Unit Most teachers will present the two investigations in this unit sequentially. However, the second investigation is not dependent on the first; they can be done in either order and at different times during the year. For example, you might use one investigation earlier in the year as a short break between longer units, and do the other investigation later in the year. If you have regular access to computers, either on the computers in the classroom or in the computer lab, you may want to do the second investigation, Paths and *Geo-Logo*, first and earlier in the school year, so that students have enough time to become familiar with the *Geo-Logo* software.

Depending on the needs and interests of your students, many of the activities in these investigations can be extended and expanded.

Connections with Other Units If you are doing the full-year *Investigations* curriculum in the suggested sequence for grade 2, this is the sixth of eight units. The work in this unit complements the work in the unit *Shapes, Halves, and Symmetry*. Students continue their work on computers and are introduced to the computer program *Geo-Logo*.

This unit can also be used successfully at grade 1, depending on the previous experience and needs of your students.

Investigations Curriculum ■ Suggested Grade 2 Sequence

Mathematical Thinking at Grade 2 (Introduction)

Coins, Coupons, and Combinations (The Number System)

Does It Walk, Crawl, or Swim? (Sorting and Classifying Data)

Shapes, Halves, and Symmetry (Geometry and Fractions)

Putting Together and Taking Apart (Addition and Subtraction)

▶ *How Long? How Far?* (Measuring)

How Many Pockets? How Many Teeth ? (Collecting and Representing Data)

Timelines and Rhythm Patterns (Representing Time)

Investigation 1 ▪ Comparing Lengths

Class Sessions	Activities	Pacing
Session 1 (p. 5) SCAVENGER HUNT	Scavenger Hunt 1: Matching Lengths Introducing Math Folders and Weekly Logs Homework: Finding Similar Lengths	minimum 1 hr
Sessions 2, 3, and 4 (p. 12) A SCAVENGER HUNT CHOICE TIME	Scavenger Hunt 2: How Many Paper Strips? On-Computer Activity: Introducing Steps Choice Time Class Discussion: Scavenger Hunt 1—Matching Lengths Homework: Scavenger Hunt	minimum 3 hr
Sessions 5, 6, and 7 (p. 28) CHOICES ABOUT MEASUREMENT	How Far Can You Jump? Measurement Riddles On-Computer Activity: Giant Steps Choice Time Class Discussion: Scavenger Hunt 2— How Many Paper Strips? Class Discussion: Choice Time Activities Homework: Measuring at Home Homework: Measurement Riddles Extension: Using Related Units	minimum 3 hr
Session 8 (p. 37) MEASURING OUR CLASSROOM	Assessment: Measuring Our Classroom Class Discussion: Measuring Our Classroom	minimum 1 hr

Start-Up ▪ Today's Number

Mathematical Emphasis

- Using direct and indirect comparison to compare lengths

- Using a nonstandard unit to measure length

- Comparing the effects of measurement using units of different size

- Communicating the need for using a standard unit

Assessment Resources

Observing the Students (p. 7)

Finding Equivalent Lengths (Teacher Note, p. 10)

Observing the Students (p. 18)

Teacher Checkpoint: Scavenger Hunt 2: How Many Paper Strips? (p. 18)

Keeping Track of Students' Work (Teacher Note, p. 25)

Matching Lengths (Dialogue Box, p. 26)

Using Related Units of Measure (Dialogue Box, p. 27)

Observing the Students (p. 33)

Assessment: Measuring Our Classroom (p. 37)

Combining, Comparing, and Measuring (Teacher Note, p. 41)

How Wide Is Our Classroom? (Dialogue Box, p. 43)

Materials

Nonstandard measuring materials (craft sticks, paper clips, straws, etc.)

Interlocking cubes

String or ribbon

Student math folders

Adding machine tape

Chart paper

Blue construction paper or index cards

Yellow construction paper or index cards

Game pieces or place markers

Computers

Geo-Logo software

Large-screen monitor or projection device

Masking tape

Family letter

Scissors

Student Sheets 1–10

Teaching resource sheet

Investigation 2 ▪ Paths and *Geo-Logo*

Class Sessions	Activities	Pacing
Session 1 (p. 47) WALKING, VISUALIZING, AND REPRESENTING PATHS	Introducing Paths Walking Paths in the Classroom Walking and Drawing Paths Homework: A Neighborhood Path Extension: Walking a Path in Our School	minimum 1 hr
Sessions 2 and 3 (p. 54) INVESTIGATING TURNS	Turning Your Body On-Computer Activity: Introducing Maze Turning Turtles Choice Time Homework: Walking a Path at Home	minimum 2 hr
Sessions 4 and 5 (p. 63) MEASURING PATHS	Comparing Lengths of Paths Introducing Paper Paths On-Computer Activity: More About Maze Choice Time Homework: Today's Number	minimum 2 hr
Sessions 6, 7, and 8 (p. 70) MOVING ON A GRID	Andy the Ant Introducing Allison's Travels On-Computer Activity: Introducing Tina the Turtle Choice Time Class Discussion: Choice Time Activities Choosing Student Work to Save Homework: Three Paths for Andy the Ant	minimum 3 hr
Ongoing Excursion* (p. 79) *GEO-LOGO:* SHAPES AND PICTURES	On-Computer Activity: Shapes and Pictures	

Start-Up ▪ **Today's Number, How Many Pockets?**

*Excursions can be omitted without harming the integrity or continuity of the unit, but offer good mathematical work if you have time to include them.

Mathematical Emphasis	Assessment Resources	Materials
▪ Moving along a path ▪ Visualizing and then representing a path ▪ Determining path length by iterating and counting units ▪ Comparing lengths of paths by comparing the number of units used to measure each path	Walking and Drawing Paths (Dialogue Box, p. 52) Observing the Students (p. 60) Observing the Students (p. 68) Teacher Checkpoint: Making and Comparing Paper Paths (p. 68) Comparing Lengths of Paths (Dialogue Box, p. 69) Observing the Students (p. 71) Observing the Students (p. 75) Choosing Student Work to Save (p. 78)	Drawing paper Crayons or markers Chalk Clipboards Adding machine tape Carpet remnants, traffic cones, or poster board geometric shapes Masking tape Red construction paper Computers *Geo-Logo* software Overhead projector Student Sheets 11–24 Teaching resource sheets

Following are the basic materials needed for the activities in this unit. Many of the items can be purchased from the publisher, either individually or in the Teacher Resource Package and the Student Materials Kit for grade 2. Detailed information is available on the *Investigations* order form. To obtain this form, call toll-free 1-800-872-1100 and ask for a Dale Seymour customer service representative.

Computers: Macintosh II or above, with 4 MB of internal memory (RAM) and Apple System Software 7.0 or later. (see the **Teacher Note**, Managing the Computer Activities, p. 22): 1–5 computers

Apple Macintosh disk, *Geo-Logo* (packaged with this book)

A projection device or large-screen monitor on one computer for whole-class viewing (optional)

Snap™ Cubes (interlocking cubes): at least 30 per student

String (or ribbon): 2–4 rolls

4"-by-6" index cards (blue): 1–2 packages

3"-by-5" index cards (yellow): 1–2 packages

Adding machine tape: 6–8 rolls

Masking tape: 6–8 rolls

Collection of classroom objects (for measuring)

4-inch craft sticks (for measuring): 200–300

Straws (for measuring): 2–4 boxes (optional)

Small paper clips (for measuring): 4–6 boxes of 100

Game or place markers such as cubes, pennies, and paper clips

Drawing paper

9"-by-12" construction paper (red)

Chart paper

Overhead projector

Folders for student work: 1 per student

Scissors

Crayons, markers

Sidewalk chalk (optional)

Clipboards (optional)

Carpet remnants/traffic cones (for creating paths, optional)

The following materials are provided at the end of this unit as blackline masters. A Student Activity Booklet containing all student sheets and teaching resources needed for individual work is available.

Family Letter (p. 134)

Student Sheets 1–24 (p. 135)

Teaching Resources:

    Turtle Turners (p. 159)

    Turtle Turner Pointers (p. 160)

    Geo-Logo User Sheet (p. 161)

Practice Pages (p. 163)

Related Children's Literature

Guiberson, Brenda. *Cactus Hotel*. New York: Henry Holt, 1991.

Lionni, Leo. *Inch by Inch*. New York: Astor-Honor, 1960.

Mahy, Margaret. *Jam*. Boston: The Atlantic Monthly Press, 1985.

Pigdon, Keith, and Marilyn Wooley. *How Far Can You Jump?* New York: Macmillan, 1987.

Russo, Marisabina. *The Line Up Book*. New York: Greenwillow Books, 1986.

Young children are often curious about and interested in questions of measurement. It is not unusual to see children comparing heights to find out who is taller. Nor is it unusual to hear students asking "Who is the oldest? How much older?" or commenting about the size of dinosaurs, whales, and even goldfish and tadpoles. However, young students need many opportunities to develop their understanding of the particular attribute they are comparing or measuring. This conceptual development is important for any attribute we measure, whether it is length, area, volume, weight, or even time.

In this unit, students develop their understanding of the concept of length. As they compare lengths of real-world objects, they come to recognize length in many different contexts. For instance, talking about length seems straightforward when we are considering the length of a pencil or a straight line. It becomes more complex, however, when we are talking about a three-dimensional object like a desk—a desktop has length and width. Since both of these dimensions have length, we can compare or measure the *length* of each dimension. Think about the many line segments we could find in, say, a bookcase—top to bottom, corner to corner, front to back. Each of these segments has a length; which we measure depends on our purpose.

How do students compare lengths of objects? Some students compare objects directly by placing them side by side. Others compare indirectly by introducing a third object such as a string. They might compare two objects that cannot be placed next to each other by cutting a string to be the length of one object, then comparing the length of that string to the other object. As students gain experience with length, these methods of comparison give way to the more sophisticated strategy of using nonstandard units. Students actually measure using nonstandard units, such as interlocking cubes. Students join the cubes (or repeatedly place the nonstandard units end to end) and count how many unit lengths "fit" in the length of an object. This method is more sophisticated because it introduces the power of numerical reasoning to thinking about length. A continuous length is now countable—the number of discrete units that equal the continuous length can

be counted. This is much more powerful than direct or indirect comparison of length. Numerous objects in various locations can be numerically compared. Total lengths, as well as differences in length, can be found. And lengths can be verbally described and permanently recorded.

In the second part of the unit, students bring their understanding of length to a new context, paths. As students walk paths in the classroom, find lengths of paths, and direct the turtle's movements using the *Geo-Logo* software, their notions of length are extended from the static context of examining objects to the dynamic context of motion. Because a path can be considered a record of movement, thinking about lengths of paths gives students a way to make sense of the important notion of distance traveled. For example, to determine the distance a student travels from home to school, he or she can measure the length of the path walked. Even more sophisticated thinking is developed as students solve problems requiring them to plan complex paths that pass through specified locations and satisfy given distance requirements. As students work with *Geo-Logo* on the computer, they must consider the length of the path the turtle must make to reach a target, travel through a maze, or construct a shape.

At the beginning of each investigation, the Mathematical Emphasis section tells you what is most important for students to learn about during that investigation. Many of these understandings and processes are difficult and complex. Students gradually learn more and more about each idea over many years of schooling. Individual students will begin and end the unit with different levels of knowledge and skill, but all will gain greater knowledge of the concept of length and develop strategies for comparing and describing lengths of objects and paths.

Throughout the *Investigations* curriculum, there are many opportunities for ongoing daily assessment as you observe, listen to, and interact with students at work. In this unit, you will find two Teacher Checkpoints:

> Investigation 1, Sessions 2–4:
> Choice Time: Scavenger Hunt 2 (p. 18)
>
> Investigation 2, Sessions 4–5:
> Choice Time: Making and Comparing Paper Paths (p. 68)

This unit also has one embedded assessment activities:

> Investigation 1, Session 8:
> Measuring Our Classroom (p. 37)

In addition, you can use almost any activity in this unit to assess your students' needs and strengths. Listed below are questions to help you focus your observation in each investigation. You may want to keep track of your observations for each student to help you plan your curriculum and monitor students' growth. Suggestions for documenting student growth can be found in the section About Assessment.

Investigation 1: Comparing Lengths

■ How do students make direct comparisons of length? Do they estimate? What strategies do students invent for making indirect comparisons? For example, do they cut a length of string to match an item and compare the lengths?

■ How do students use nonstandard units to compare lengths? Do they line units up end to end? Do they leave gaps between units? Do they overlap units? Do they repeatedly place only one unit along each length, keeping track of how many times they do so?

■ How do students relate measurements made with different units? Do they view measuring an object with two different units as two unrelated tasks? Do they use the relationship between two different units to estimate how those units would fit along an object? Do they view this relationship as a numerical or a spatial one? Do students know that measuring with a small unit will require more units than measuring with a larger unit?

■ What do students say about the need for a standard unit for measuring length? How do they explain different measurements based on different, nonstandard units of measure?

Investigation 2: Paths and *Geo-Logo*

■ How do students describe movements along a path? What language do they use?

■ How do students visualize paths? How do they describe paths (turns, landmarks, straight stretches) before they walk them? as they walk them? Does describing a path as they walk it help them to visualize or describe the path afterward? How do they represent paths? Do they use landmarks? Do they include all parts of the paths? Do they show turns?

■ How do students place a unit along a path to measure it? Do they overlap or leave gaps between units? How do they find the length of the path? Do they count units accurately?

■ How do students compare the lengths of paths? Do they compare the number of units in each? Do they focus on the distance between the starting and ending points without attending to the path in between? Do they realize that the shortest path between two points will have no turns?

In the *Investigations* curriculum, mathematical vocabulary is introduced naturally during the activities. We don't ask students to learn definitions of new terms; rather, they come to understand such words as *factor* or *area* or *symmetry* by hearing them used frequently in discussion as they investigate new concepts. This approach is compatible with current theories of second-language acquisition, which emphasize the use of new vocabulary in meaningful contexts while students are actively involved with objects, pictures, and physical movement.

Listed below are some key words used in this unit that will not be new to most English speakers at this age level but may be unfamiliar to students with limited English proficiency. You will want to spend additional time working on these words with your students who are learning English. If your students are working with a second-language teacher, you might enlist your colleague's aid in familiarizing students with these words before and during this unit. In the classroom, look for opportunities for students to hear and use these words. Activities you can use to present the words are given in the appendix, Vocabulary Support for Second-Language Learners (p. 91).

matching, length, long, farther, farthest, closest, distance Students measure objects and distances in the classroom by finding objects that are about the same as a given length and by using nonstandard units to find things that are a certain number of units long.

straight, turn, path, left, right Students will encounter these terms as they follow paths and describe paths taken by the turtle on the *Geo-Logo* software.

Multicultural Extensions for All Students

Whenever possible, encourage students to share words, objects, customs, or any aspects of daily life from their own cultures and backgrounds that are relevant to the activities in this unit. For example:

■ Students who have lived in or visited other countries may be familiar with the metric system. Encourage them to describe terms that are used to measure length or distance (such as *centime-ter, meter, kilometer*). Students may recall experiences measuring with a centimeter ruler or a meterstick or seeing road signs with the term *kilometer*.

■ Begin a collection of empty food containers or other boxes that include a metric unit of measure. As students bring these containers from home, make a list of the different terms and talk about their meanings. Students can sort the containers by types of measures.

Investigations

Comparing Lengths

What Happens

Session 1: Scavenger Hunt Students find items that are *about* the same length as each of several strips of adding machine tape that are posted around the room. They compare the length of the items with the length of the strips, and for each length, record the items they find that match.

Sessions 2, 3, and 4: A Scavenger Hunt Choice Time Students work on three activities in Choice Time over the three sessions. They use nonstandard units to find things that are a certain number of units long, then predict and measure how long those items are when a related nonstandard unit is used. This activity is used as a Teacher Checkpoint. Students are also introduced to Steps, a computer activity in which the *Geo-Logo* turtle is moved by unit lengths.

Sessions 5, 6, and 7: Choices About Measurement Students are introduced to three additional choices. In How Far Can You Jump? and Measurement Riddles they measure and compare lengths. In Giant Steps, a computer activity, they move a "turtle" by different-sized unit lengths. Scavenger Hunt 2: How Many Paper Strips?, is another choice for these sessions. A class discussion at the end of Session 7 gives students the opportunity to talk about and reflect on their work.

Session 8: Measuring Our Classroom As an assessment, students use units of their own choosing to measure the width of the classroom. As a class, they discuss the variety of measures they found.

Mathematical Emphasis

- Using direct and indirect comparison to compare lengths
- Using a nonstandard unit to measure length
- Comparing the effects of measurement using units of different size
- Communicating the need for using a standard unit

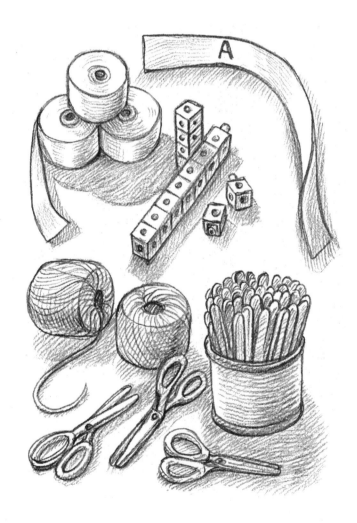

What to Plan Ahead of Time

Materials

- Materials that can be used as nonstandard units of measure, such as craft sticks, paper clips, straws: enough to measure the length or width of your classroom (all sessions)

- Interlocking cubes: about 30 per student (all sessions)

- String or ribbon: 2–3 rolls. Yarn is not recommended because it stretches easily. (Sessions 1–4)

- Student math folders: 1 per student (Session 1)

- Adding machine tape: 3–6 rolls (all sessions)

- Chart paper (Sessions 1–5, 8)

- 6″ blue paper strips cut from blue index cards or construction paper: 5 per student (Sessions 2–8)

- 3″ yellow paper strips cut from yellow index cards or construction paper: 10 per student (Sessions 2–8)

- Game or place markers such as cubes, pennies, and paper clips (Sessions 5–7)

- Computers: Macintosh II or above, with 4 MB of internal memory (RAM) and Apple System Software 7.0 or later: 1 per 4–6 students (Sessions 2–7)

- A projection device or large-screen monitor on one computer for whole-class viewing (Sessions 2–7, optional)

- Apple Macintosh disk, *Geo-Logo* (Sessions 2–7)

- Masking tape (Sessions 2–7)

- Scissors (Session 5)

Other Preparation

- Duplicate student sheets and teaching resources (located at the end of this unit) in the following quantities. If you have Student Activity Booklets, copy only the items marked with an asterisk.

For Session 1

Student Sheet 1, Weekly Log (p. 135): 1 per student. At this time, you may wish to duplicate a supply to last for the entire unit and distribute the sheets as needed.

Student Sheets 2 and 3, Scavenger Hunt 1 (pp. 136–137): 1 each per student

Student Sheet 4, Finding Similar Lengths (p. 138): 1 per student (homework)

Family letter* (p. 134): 1 per student. Remember to sign and date the letter before copying it.

For Sessions 2–4

Student Sheet 5, Scavenger Hunt 2 (p. 139): 1 per student (class), 1 per student (homework)

Geo-Logo User Sheet* (p. 161): Post one copy beside each computer.

Student Sheet 6, Scavenger Hunt 2 (p. 140): 1 per student

Student Sheet 7, Measuring Strips (p. 141): 1 per student (homework), plus extras*

For Sessions 5–7

Student Sheet 8, How Far Can You Jump? (p. 142): 1 per student

Continued on next page

Student Sheet 9, Measuring at Home
(p. 143): 1 per student (homework)

Student Sheet 10, Measurement Riddles
(p. 144): 1 per student (homework)

■ Cut two or more identical sets of 6 strips of
adding machine tape in lengths that match
items in your classroom. For example, you
might cut strips the length of a book, the
height of a wastebasket, the width of a table
or desk, the width of a window, the length
of a bookshelf, and the height of a bookcase.
You will need a variety of lengths. The
lengths should vary by at least 10–12 inches.
Label the strips A through F. Post the strips
horizontally in different areas of the classroom at a height accessible to students.
(Session 1)

■ Prepare a math folder for each student if
you did not do so for a previous unit.
(Session 1)

■ Cut 6"-by-1" blue paper strips and 3"-by-1"
yellow paper strips from index cards or construction paper. Prepare enough strips so
that each pair has 5 blue and 20 yellow
strips, and you have a few extras. Strips can
be easily prepared by cutting colored index
cards. The 6" strips can be cut from 4"-by-
6" index cards in one color, and the 3" strips
can be cut from 3"-by-5" index cards in
another color. Or, you can cut the strips
from two different colors of construction
paper. (Sessions 2–4)

■ Gather about 6 classroom objects, one or
two of which are about 6" long (such as a
pen, a marker, a book). (Sessions 2–4)

■ Install *Geo-Logo* on each computer. (See
p. 129 of the *Geo-Logo* Teacher Tutorial.)
See the **Teacher Note**, Managing the
Computer Activities (p. 22), for suggestions
about how to incorporate the computer
activities into the curriculum depending on
the number of computers available to you.
(Sessions 2–4)

■ Work through the *Geo-Logo* Teacher Tutorial
(p. 93) and try the activities yourself before
introducing them to students. (Sessions 2–4)

■ Set up two (or three) areas in the classroom
or hallway where students can jump. Use
masking tape to make a starting line 4 to 6
feet long. Place masking tape and pencils
and containers of markers such as cubes,
pennies, and paper clips in each area.
(Sessions 5–7)

■ Using interlocking cubes, measure the
length (or width, or height) of four to six
classroom objects. Use the measurements to
create Measurement Riddles. Some examples (a bulletin board and a square table)
are provided here. Other possibilities may
include smaller items such as a calendar, a
poster or picture, a fish tank, a favorite children's book, or a piece of drawing paper.
(Sessions 5–7)

I am a very big rectangle.	I have a square top.
I am 80 cubes long.	I am 64 cubes long.
I am 48 cubes tall.	I am 64 cubes wide.
What could I be?	What could I be?

Write each riddle on large paper and post
the riddles in the classroom, or prepare a
sheet with several riddles for each student.

■ Measure in cubes the length and width of
your classroom calendar (or any other rec-
tangular object hanging on a wall) for the
measurement riddle given on p. 31.
(Sessions 5–7)

Scavenger Hunt

What Happens

Students find items that are *about* the same length as each of several strips of adding machine tape that are posted around the room. They compare the length of the items with the length of the strips, and for each length, record the items they find that match. Their work focuses on:

■ finding a way to compare two lengths

■ using direct and indirect comparison to identify equal lengths

Start-Up

Today's Number Today's Number is one of the routines that are built into the grade 2 *Investigations* curriculum. Routines provide students regular practice in important mathematical ideas such as number combinations, counting and estimating data, and concepts of time. For Today's Number, which is done daily (or most days), students write number sentences that equal the number of days they have been in school. The complete description of Today's Number (p. 82) offers suggestions for establishing this routine and some variations.

If you are doing the full-year grade 2 *Investigations* curriculum, you will have already started a 200 chart and a counting strip during the unit *Mathematical Thinking at Grade 2*. Write the next number on the 200 chart and add the next number card to the counting strip. As a class, brainstorm ways to express the number.

If you are teaching an *Investigations* unit for the first time, here are a few options for incorporating Today's Number as a routine:

■ **Begin with 1** Begin a counting line that does not correspond to the school day number. Each day add a number to the strip and use this number as Today's Number.

■ **Use the Calendar Date** If today is the sixteenth day of the month, use 16 as Today's Number.

After Today's Number has been established, ask students to think about different ways to write the number. Post a piece of chart paper to record their suggestions. You might want to offer ideas to help students get started. If Today's Number is 45, you might suggest 40 + 5 or 20 + 25.

Ask students to think about other ways to make Today's Number. List their suggestions on chart paper. As students offer suggestions, occasionally ask the group if they agree with the statements. In this way, students have the opportunity to confirm an idea that they had or to respond to an incorrect suggestion.

Materials

■ Prepared strips of adding machine tape

■ Rolls of adding machine tape

■ String or ribbon (several rolls)

■ Interlocking cubes (about 30 per student)

■ Other nonstandard measuring units such as craft sticks (200–300)

■ Chart paper

■ Student math folders (1 per student)

■ Student Sheet 1 (1 per student)

■ Student Sheets 2 and 3 (1 of each per student)

■ Family letter (1 per student)

■ Student Sheet 4 (1 per student, homework)

As students grow more accustomed to this routine, they will begin to see patterns in the combinations, have favorite kinds of number sentences, or use more complicated types of expressions. Today's Number can be recorded daily on the Weekly Log. (See p. 8.)

(See p. 8.)

Activity

Scavenger Hunt 1: Matching Lengths

Point out the strips of adding machine tape you have posted around the classroom.

Look at the paper strips I have displayed around the room. What can you tell about the strips just by looking at them?

Franco thinks that this strip over here is the shortest one, and Linda said she thinks that all of the strips are different lengths. The strips *are* all different lengths, and we're going to use them in a scavenger hunt. You will work with partners to find things in the classroom that are about the same length as each strip.

You might want to explain that a scavenger hunt is a game where people find different things that are on a list. Then point out one strip (choose a longer one), and ask students to suggest some things that might be the same length as the strip.

Yes, the length of the bookcase, the width of the classroom door, or the length of the computer table *might* be the same length as this paper strip. Your job will be to find things in the classroom that are about the same length as the strips. You cannot move the strips—the strips are to stay where I have put them—but you can use materials in the classroom to help you.

Emphasize that items students find for each strip should be *about* the same length as the strips; they do not have to be exactly the same lengths. To help students develop a sense of what *about the same length* means, compare the lengths of two objects to one of the strips you have posted. Make the length of one object clearly different from that of the strip, while the other object is about the same length as the strip.

As you talk about this, explain to students that they will work with partners to find a way to compare the length (or width) of things in the classroom to the strips. Students may have ideas or questions about materials they can use as they look for objects to match the strips. You might suggest string, adding machine tape, interlocking cubes, or another manipulative. Ask students to find items for at least three of the strips.

Provide students with Student Sheets 2 and 3, Scavenger Hunt 1. Discuss these recording sheets, asking students to record in the corresponding spaces the objects they find to match each strip's length. Students can describe the strategies they used on the bottom of Student Sheet 3.

For information about methods of comparing lengths see the **Teacher Note**, Finding Equivalent Lengths (p. 10).

Observing the Students As you circulate among students, note how they are comparing the lengths of the strips with the lengths of the objects.

■ How do students compare lengths to the shortest strips? Direct comparison may be many students' method of choice for short lengths. Students can easily hold a book, paintbrush, or sheet of paper alongside short strips to compare lengths.

■ How do students compare longer lengths? Do they invent indirect comparison strategies? For example, do they cut a length of string that matches a long strip and use it to compare the strip and another length?

- Do students use nonstandard units to compare lengths? For instance, do they measure a strip in interlocking cubes, then use the cube train to find equal lengths or measure objects in cubes and compare lengths? If students use other, noncontinuous units, such as craft sticks, note how they use these units. Do they line units end to end? Do they leave gaps between units, or overlap units? Do they repeatedly place only one unit along each length, keeping track of how many times they do so?
- Are students flexible in their use of materials and methods? Do they use strategies that "fit" the task? For example, for short lengths, direct comparison often works well and may be more efficient than indirect comparison or using nonstandard units.

Note: Leave the strips posted, as students can continue this activity during Choice Time in Sessions 2, 3, and 4.

Activity

Introducing Math Folders and Weekly Logs

If you are using the full-year *Investigations* curriculum, students will be familiar with math folders and Weekly Logs. If this curriculum is new to students, tell them about one way they will keep track of the math work they do.

Mathematicians show how they think about and solve problems by talking about their work, drawing pictures, building models, and explaining their work in writing so that they can share their ideas with other people. Your math folder will be a place to collect the writing and drawing that you do in math class.

Distribute a math folder to students and have them label it with their names.

Your math folder is a place to keep track of what you do each day in math class. Sometimes there will be more than one activity to choose from, and at other times, like today, everyone in the class will do the same thing. Each day you will also record what you did on this Weekly Log.

Students should put Student Sheets 2 and 3 into their folders. Distribute Student Sheet 1, Weekly Log, and ask students to write their name at the top of the page. Point out that there are spaces for each day of the week and ask them to write today's date on the line after the appropriate day. If you are doing the activity Today's Number, students can write the number in the box beside the date.

Ask students for suggestions about what to call today's activity. Titles for choices and whole-class activities should be short to encourage all students to record what they do each day. List their ideas on the board or on chart paper and have students choose one title to write in the space below the date.

❖ **Tip for the Linguistically Diverse Classroom** Encourage students who are not writing comfortably in English to use drawings to record in their Weekly Log. If students demonstrate some proficiency in writing, suggest that they record a few words with their drawings. Students can also record a sample problem representative of each day's work.

Weekly Logs can be stapled to the front of the folders (each new week on the top so that students can view prior logs by lifting up the sheets).

During the unit, or through the year, you might use the math folders and Weekly Logs in a number of ways:

- to keep track of what kinds of activities students choose to do and how frequently they choose them
- to review with students, individually or as a group, the work they've accomplished
- to share student work with families, either by sending logs and/or folders home periodically for students to share or during student/family/teacher conferences.

Session 1 Follow-Up

Finding Similar Lengths Each student chooses one thing at home or in the neighborhood and finds a different item that is about the same length. Students draw or write about what they compared and the strategy they used on Student Sheet 4, Finding Similar Lengths.

 **Homework**

Send home the family letter or the *Investigations* at Home booklet.

When students are attempting to find objects that are the same length as the paper strips in the scavenger hunt, they use variations of three methods.

Students directly compare by placing an object against a strip to see if both have the same length. Of course, students must decide which dimension of an object to compare to a strip. They may compare one dimension of an object to a strip—for example, the length of a book—but if the lengths don't match, they discard the object and go on to a different one. Because students may focus on one dimension and not consider different dimensions of an object, such as the book's width, they may not think about turning the object and comparing another of its dimensions as a possibility.

Students indirectly compare an object to a strip by using a third object, such as a string, to compare lengths. For instance, a student might visually search the room for an object that looks the same length as a given strip. Once an object is located, the student might cut a piece of string the same length as a given dimension of the object. The student then compares that string to the strip. A more efficient strategy would be to cut a piece of string the same length as the strip, then walk around the room comparing the string to various objects.

Students use repeated units to measure the lengths of objects by counting how many unit lengths "fit" in each and then compare these counts. For instance, a student might find that one strip is three pencils long, then find an object in the classroom that is three pencils long.

There are, however, various degrees of sophistication with this method. Some students can use this method only if they have enough unit lengths to place end to end for the entire length of the object. Other students can use a single object and iterate it— that is, place it along the length of an object, mark its end, then pick it up and place the length again, this time starting at its previous endpoint, and so on.

You may see students using various degrees of care in their unit iterations. Some may use their hands to iterate but pay little attention to whether their hands are oriented the same way each time (so the length measured is always the same) or whether there are any gaps or overlaps in their hands' placement. Some may even think that several students' hands can be used, even though the hands are of different sizes. Such actions indicate that students, although beginning to understand the process of unit iteration, are unaware of a critical feature of iteration, namely, that we must count how many times a *single unit* must be used to completely cover, with no gaps or overlaps, the length of an object.

As students work, ask questions to encourage them to reflect on the reliability of their iteration strategies. The questions included here help students see that a unit must be used in a consistent way (for example, hands placed horizontally as opposed to horizontally *and* vertically) and carefully iterated. If not, they may get different measurements for the same object, even though they are measuring with the same unit. This can't be very accurate. For instance, if students get 12 hands when they measure a strip one time, but 8 hands when they measure it the second time, how can these numbers help them find an object the same length as the strip? How many hands long will the object have to be? 8? 12? 10? To help students think about this, ask:

Do you always get the same number when you measure the desk with your hands? Should you? Why?

Do you get the same number if you hold your hands this way [*oriented vertically*] and this way [*oriented horizontally*]? Why not? So what do you have to remember if you measure something with your hands?

Continued on next page

The process of measuring length is more complex than it may initially seem. When students measure length, they are, in effect, separating a continuous distance into countable units. This is essentially the function of linear measurement tools, such as inch sticks, rulers, and yardsticks. However, students need many experiences using nonstandard materials to construct understanding of the process of measurement before they are able to meaningfully use measuring tools. They need opportunities to choose appropriate units for measuring length—units that match the attribute of length, such as craft sticks, file card strips, and paper clips—and experiences lining up and counting units, or iterating a single unit, to measure length.

As students' understanding of measurement develops, they begin to formulate ideas about the need for a standard measuring tool, such as a ruler or yardstick. This is a time when using measuring tools becomes meaningful for students, and it is based on the conceptual understanding students develop through many experiences using nonstandard units to measure. The need for a standard measuring tool is among the topics in measurement students investigate in the *Investigations* curriculum at grade 3, in the unit *From Paces to Feet*.

A Scavenger Hunt Choice Time

Materials

- Prepared strips of adding machine tape (from Session 1)
- Masking tape
- String or ribbon (several rolls)
- Interlocking cubes (about 30 per student)
- 4 to 6 objects
- 6" blue paper strips (5 per pair)
- 3" yellow paper strips (20 per pair)
- Computers with *Geo-Logo* installed
- Student Sheet 5 (1 per student, class; 1 per student, homework)
- Student Sheet 6 (1 per student)
- Student Sheet 7 (1 per student, homework, plus extras)
- *Geo-Logo* User Sheet (1 for each computer)
- Chart paper

What Happens

Students work on three activities in Choice Time over the three sessions. They use nonstandard units to find things that are a certain number of units long, then predict and measure how long those items are when a related nonstandard unit is used. This activity is used as a Teacher Checkpoint. Students are also introduced to Steps, a computer activity in which the *Geo-Logo* turtle is moved by unit lengths. Their work focuses on:

- using direct and indirect comparison to identify equal lengths
- learning to iterate units
- seeing that units can be related and that when you know how long something is in one unit, you can figure out its length in a related unit

Start-Up

Today's Number

- **Calendar Date**   If you are using the calendar date for Today's Number, brainstorm with students ways to express the number. Suggest students include subtraction as a way to express the number. Record students' expressions on chart paper so that they can be saved each day.

- **Number of School Days**   If you are using the number of school days for Today's Number, and the number is over 100, encourage students to break apart the number (132 = 100 + 32) and then offer suggestions to express one of those numbers, keeping the other intact. For example: 100 + 16 + 16 or 100 + 10 + 10 + 10 + 2. Add a card to the class counting strip and fill in another number on the blank 200 chart.

For a complete discussion of this routine, see p. 82.

Homework   Ask students to describe two items they found at home that are about the same length and tell what strategy they used to compare.

Scavenger Hunt 2: How Many Paper Strips?

Note: This activity is introduced to students here and continued as a Choice Time activity. It will be used as a Teacher Checkpoint, a time for you to pause and reflect on your teaching plan, observe students at work, and get an overall sense of how your class is doing in the unit. This Teacher Checkpoint provides an opportunity to look carefully at how students are thinking about and using nonstandard units. Guidelines for what to look for are provided in Observing the Students (p. 18).

Post a 6" blue paper strip and a 3" yellow paper strip side by side on the chalkboard. The objects you will use and blue and yellow strips should be accessible.

Remind students of the work they did in the first scavenger hunt activity. Then introduce the second scavenger hunt.

In this activity, you will work with a partner to find things that are a certain number of blue strips long. For example, you might have to find something that is 10 blue strips long, or something that is 3 blue strips long. What you need to find is listed on your student sheet.

When you've found an object that matches the number of blue strips, write or draw a picture of it on your student sheet. Then predict how many yellow strips long it will be, write your prediction, and measure to check. Remember to predict how many yellow strips before you use them to measure.

Distribute Student Sheets 5 and 6, Scavenger Hunt 2 to each student and work through one example together. From your collection of objects, have students find an item that is 1 blue strip long, predict how many yellow strips long it will be, and then measure to check. Talk with students about how to record the objects they found, their predictions, and their measurements.

. . . .

❖ **Tip for the Linguistically Diverse Classroom**   It may help students with limited English proficiency to put rebuses over the words *predict* and *measure* as they work on the student sheets. Suggest students draw a question mark over each word *predict* and a paper strip over each word *measure*. Then ask students to draw what they find.

. . . .

Some problems require more blue strips than pairs of students have. Encourage students to find things that are 6, 7, and 10 blue strips long *without* using strips of another pair of students. These problems help students to move away from lining up units end to end and to move toward repeatedly iterating a unit of measure.

Students will continue this activity during Choice Time. If they do not finish it during Sessions 2, 3, and 4, they will have an additional opportunity to work on it along with two other choices during Sessions 5, 6, and 7.

On-Computer Activity: Introducing Steps

Note: Work through the Steps activity in the *Geo-Logo* Teacher Tutorial (p. 97) before working on the computer with students. Post copies of the *Geo-Logo* User Sheet, next to each computer. Also read the **Teacher Note**, Spatial Sense and Geometry with *Geo-Logo* (p. 23), for information about how this software contributes to students' learning in mathematics.

If you have computers available, it is highly recommended that you use the *Geo-Logo* software. The computer work is integrated into the unit and enriches the work students do. In this activity, students work in pairs. Each student tries to get the turtle from the bottom of the screen, the starting point, to a target object.

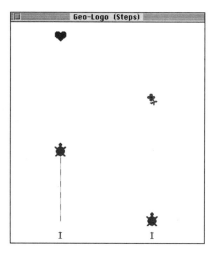

Introduce the computer game to the whole class with a computer and a projection device for screen display. If you do not have a projection device, gather students around the largest monitor available, or introduce the game to small groups of students. Demonstrate how to:

- turn on the computer.
- open *Geo-Logo* by double-clicking on the turtle icon.
- open Steps by clicking on it once.

Read the directions, then click on **[OK]** or press **<return>**. Two turtles, each facing a target object, appear. Students work in pairs to move the turtle to a target by estimating and entering numbers of units.

Explain that the goal is to get the turtle to the target with the fewest possible commands. The target shapes are directly in front of each turtle. The unit length for the turtles (how far they go forward with each "step") is a line segment that is shown just below the turtle. Students first click on the turtle they wish to move (this may generate a t a l k t o command in the Command Center; if the turtle they click on is already the "active turtle"— t u r t l e 1 on the left—no command needs to be generated). They then type a forward command, which is the letter "f", a space, and a number, and then press return. For example, f **<space>** 1 2 **<return>** would move the turtle 12 steps forward. If the turtle reaches the target, the target object grows and shrinks. To reach a target, the turtle must stop directly on top of it.

Ask students what command to enter for t u r t l e 1, the turtle on the left, to get to the target. As you type it in, announce every key you press.

We want to go forward 12 turtle steps, so I'll type f <space> 1 2 and then press <return>.

Pretend I am the partner now. I want to move t u r t l e 2.

Using the mouse, click on t u r t l e 2 (turtle on the right). Point out that a t a l k t o command is automatically entered in the Command Center. As students watch, enter a command and pretend to forget to press **<return>** until the class reminds you to do so. Also, make a typing mistake and show how to use the **<delete>** key to erase a mistake.

Click on the **Erase One tool** in the Tool bar. Show students how this will erase the last command.

Discuss what to do if you enter a number so large that the turtle goes off the screen. You may want to demonstrate this. You can use the **Erase One** tool to erase the command, press **<delete>** to change the number to a smaller number, or enter a back **b** command. (For example: b **<space>** 1 0 **<return>**.)

Your partner may have clicked on a turtle and you cannot click on yours (because it's still off the screen). You can go up and change your last command or enter t1, or t2, (with the comma), which are short for "talkto turtle1" and "talkto turtle2."

Click on t u r t l e 1 and enter another forward command.

Challenge students to enter just one command that will get the turtle to the target. Ask them to explain how they figured out the commands, then try it.

Show students how to use the **Erase All tool** to begin again. The targets now have new locations. Ask students to take turns giving the first command.

Tell students that when their time on the computers is nearly up, they will need to save their work so the next time they will be able to go on from where they left off. Demonstrate how to choose **Save My Work** from the **File** menu and save the work on the computer, following the suggested procedure below.

You can save your work so you can begin where you left off the next time you use the computer. Your work will need a name so you can find it again. To name your work, include these three things:

- **the initials (or first or last names) of you and your partner(s)**
- **a short one-word name for the activity**
- **the date**

Then click on Save. For example, if Angel and Trini are working together, they could name their work "AL + TT steps 3/15." Then they can go to the File menu and choose Change Activity . . . or Quit.

Activity

Choice Time

Choice Time is a format that recurs throughout the *Investigations* curriculum. See the **Teacher Note**, About Choice Time (p. 23), for information about how to set up Choice Time, including how students might use the Weekly Log to keep track of their work.

Explain how students are to work during Choice Time. Each day they select one or two of the activities they want to participate in. Students can select the same activity more than once, but they should not do the same activity each day. Decide whether you want students to do every activity or just some of them.

List these choices on the chalkboard.

```
1. Scavenger Hunt 1

2. Scavenger Hunt 2

3. Steps (computer)
```

If Choice Time is new for your class, you may need to help students plan their activities. Assure them that they will have an opportunity to try each choice. Support students in making these decisions and plans for them-selves rather than organizing them into groups and circulating the groups. Making choices, planning time, and taking responsibility for their own learning are important aspects of a student's school experience.

Scavenger Hunt 2 is a Teacher Checkpoint; try to observe all students while they are working on this second choice.

Choice 1: Scavenger Hunt 1: Matching Lengths

Materials: Prepared strips of adding machine tape posted around the room (from Session 1), string or ribbon, interlocking cubes, Student Sheets 2 and 3, Scavenger Hunt 1.

Students find objects that are about the same length as strips of adding machine tape. Using materials such as string, ribbon, or cubes, students find ways to compare the length of the objects with the length of the strips.

Note: Students may have finished Scavenger Hunt 1 during Session 1. If not, ask them to take their papers from their math folders and complete the activity during this session so they will be able to participate in tomorrow's class discussion.

Choice 2: Scavenger Hunt 2: How Many Paper Strips?

Materials: 6" blue paper strips (5 per pair); 3" yellow paper strips (20 per pair); Student Sheets 5 and 6, Scavenger Hunt 2

Working with partners, students find objects that are a given number of blue strips long. They record the object on their student sheets, then predict how many units long it will be when it is measured with the shorter yellow paper strips. On Student Sheet 6, they record what they noticed as they used the blue and yellow strips to measure.

Note: This activity will be used as a Teacher Checkpoint. It is important that all students spend time on this activity. Suggestions on what you might look for as you observe students are given on p. 19.

Choice 3: Steps

Materials: Computers with *Geo-Logo* installed

Pairs of students take turns trying to get the turtle from the starting point at the bottom of the screen to a target object. On a turn, a student clicks on a turtle and enters a forward command to move the turtle toward its target.

Challenge students to figure out one command that will get their turtle to the target. They can use the **Erase One tool** to erase all the commands one by one and then try this new command.

Observing the Students

During this first Choice Time, observe students at work.

Do students try each choice, or do they stay with a familiar one? If, after a short time with one activity, students say they're done, ask them to tell you about what they have done and encourage them to investigate further. Do students work alone or with partners? Do they share what they have done with others and observe what others are doing? Do they talk to themselves or others about what they are doing?

The following are suggestions for what you might observe as students work on these Choice Time activities:

Scavenger Hunt 1: Matching Lengths

■ What strategies do students invent to find objects the same lengths as the paper strips?

■ Do they use direct comparison whenever possible, actually bringing each item to the strip?

■ Do they use indirect comparison—for example, cutting a length of string equal to a posted strip and then comparing the string's length to classroom objects?

■ Do students find ways to use nonstandard units to compare lengths?

Scavenger Hunt 2: How Many Paper Strips?

Use this activity as a Teacher Checkpoint by observing students as they find objects to match different numbers of strips. As you observe students measuring, spend time with students who are less experienced in measuring, offering them more items to measure.

- How do students measure with units? Do they align the end of the first strip with the edge of the item and then place the strips end to end? (For example, to measure an item 5 blue strips long, do students line up five blue strips along or on the item? If so, do the strips overlap or are there gaps between strips?)

- How do students describe lengths that include a fraction of a strip?

- How do students measure objects that take more strips than they have available?

Ask students to tell you how they are predicting how many of the smaller strips it will take to measure the length of an object.

- Do they use the 2-to-1 relationship that exists between the longer and shorter strips, and double the number used for blue strips, or count by 2's for each blue strip?

- Do they visualize how the smaller strips might fit along the item?

- Do they place one or two strips, and then predict?

- Do they treat each task as a new and different problem? (Without telling them about the 2-to-1 relationship, encourage these students to think about how many blue and yellow strips they have already used before they make their next prediction.)

See the **Dialogue Box**, Using Related Units of Measure (p. 27), for examples of students' thinking about units.

Note: As students finish, collect the blue and yellow strips. They will need these materials again for Session 8.

Steps

In this session, you will probably spend your time helping students get started and enter commands on the computer. When they ask for assistance, answer their questions and also refer them to the *Geo-Logo* User Sheet, posted next to the computer.

- What strategies do students use to estimate distances?

- Do students count without signs of iterating a unit length or use their fingers?

- Do students use a path that is already on the screen (from a partner's first attempt) to estimate the distance still needed? (This is an especially useful strategy, which students may discover as they discuss and improve their strategies for estimating distances.)

Students may go beyond the target. When this happens, the target does not change. Suggest that the student click on the **Erase One tool** and erase the last command, then enter a smaller number. Or press **<delete>** (twice to delete both digits of a two-digit number, for example), then enter a new amount. An alternative is to move the turtle backward by entering **b** and a number.

Since the goal is to reach the turtle in one or just a few commands, encourage students to combine commands. For example, if a student has used **f**, **8**, **7**, and **1** to reach the turtle, ask what single command they could use. Students can use addition strategies to combine commands, then use the **Erase One tool** or **<delete>** to erase the multiple commands and enter the single command.

Many students who are using computers and the *Geo-Logo* software for the first time will need assistance. Often students who are more familiar with computers can assist those who need help. Encourage students to experiment with the tools in *Geo-Logo* and see if they can figure out what they do and then to share what they've found. It's not unusual for students to discover things about the software that you do not know.

Near the End of the Session Five or 10 minutes before the end of each Choice Time session, have students stop working, put away the materials they have been working with, and clean up their work area.

When cleanup is complete, students should record on their Weekly Logs what they worked on during Choice Time. Suggest that they use the list of choice activities that you posted as one reference for writing about what they did.

Whenever possible, either at the beginning or end of Choice Time, have students share some of the work they have been doing. This often sparks interest in an activity. Some days you might ask two or three students to share with the class the work they have been doing. On other days you might ask a question that came up during Choice Time so that others can respond to it. Sometimes you might want students to explain how they thought about or solved a particular problem.

Activity

Class Discussion: Scavenger Hunt 1— Matching Lengths

This whole-class discussion will likely take place in Session 3 or after all students have completed Scavenger Hunt 1.

Ask students to share the objects they found for each strip. Record their responses on chart paper. Then invite students to share their strategies. Encourage them to listen closely as others explain how they compared lengths and to ask questions to be sure they understand.

If discrepancies arise, take advantage of the natural opportunity they provide for talking about the strategies students used. For instance, one student may have found that one object is the same length as Strip A, while another student found that the same object matches the length of Strip D. Different results may be due to errors in using a strategy, such as miscounting the nonstandard units used or failing to align units end to end; however, discrepancies may also arise because students have focused on different dimensions of the object. See the **Dialogue Box**, Matching Lengths (p. 26) for a discussion in one classroom about the methods students used to measure.

Post the chart of results and the corresponding paper strips in one area of the classroom. As the unit progresses students can continue to compare and add items to the list.

Note: Measure the length in interlocking cubes of several items in your classroom, and use the measurements to create measurement riddles for students to solve during Choice Time in Sessions 5, 6, and 7. For models and suggestions about measurement riddles, see Other Preparation (p. 4).

Strip A	Strip B	Strip C
book	desk	window
paintbrush	chair	game box
paper	computer	closet door
calendar	table	(across)

Strip D	Strip E	Strip F
shelf	bookcase	table
trash can		
(tall)		

A

B

C

D

E

F

Sessions 2, 3, and 4 Follow-Up

Scavenger Hunt   Students conduct a scavenger hunt at home, similar to the one they've worked on at school. They cut out (and color, if desired) the measuring strips on Student Sheet 7, Measuring Strips. They use them to conduct their hunt and record their work on a blank copy of Student Sheet 5, Scavenger Hunt 2: How Many Paper Strips?

Homework

The grade 2 *Investigations* curriculum uses two software programs developed especially for the curriculum. *Shapes* is introduced in *Mathematical Thinking at Grade 2* and used in *Shapes, Halves, and Symmetry. Geo-Logo* is introduced in *How Long? How Far?* Although the software is included in only these units, we recommend that students use the programs throughout the year. As students use the activities again and again, they develop skills and insights into important mathematical ideas.

How you use the computer activities in your classroom will depend on the number of computers you have available. Although we have included Free Explore in Choice Time activities, your computer setup may not allow student use of computers during math class. If you have a computer lab available once a week or if you have only one or two computers in your classroom, you may want to schedule student use of computers throughout the day.

Regardless of the number of computers you can use, let students work in pairs on the computer. Working in pairs not only maximizes computer resources but also encourages students to consult, monitor, and teach one another. Generally, more than two students at one computer is difficult to manage; in most such cases, one or several students will end up having limited experience with the machine and the activity. But if you have an odd number of students, you can form one threesome.

Computer Lab. If you have a computer laboratory that has one computer for each pair of students, let all the students do the computer activities at the same time. During Choice Time, students will be able to work on the other choices. Plan to have students use the computer lab for one or two periods a week.

Three to Six Computers. The curriculum is written for this case and in many ways, it is the simplest to coordinate. If you have several computers in your classroom, you can use computer activities as a Choice Time activity. You might

introduce the computer and software to the whole class, using a large-screen monitor or projection device, or to small groups gathered around a machine. Then pairs of students can cycle through the computers, just as they cycle through other choices. Each pair should spend 15 to 20 minutes at the computer in one session. It is important that every student get a chance to use the computers, so you may have to allow students to use the computers at other times of the day. Monitor computer use carefully to ensure access for all students.

One or Two Computers. If you have only one or two computers in your classroom, students will definitely need to use the computers throughout the school day so that every pair of students has sufficient opportunity to do the computer activities.

Many students who are using computers and the *Shapes* or *Geo-Logo* software for the first time will need assistance. Many of their questions will require only short answers or demonstrations. (See the Teacher Tutorial on p. 93.) You do not have to be the only source of help for these students. Often students who are more familiar with computers can assist those who need help. Encourage students to experiment and see if they can figure out what they need to do and then to share what they've discovered with each other and with you. It is not unusual for students to discover things about the software that the teacher doesn't know.

Saving Student Work Students can save their work on the computer in two ways: on the computer's internal drive or on a disk. Instructions for saving work are on p. 113 and p. 131 of the *Geo-Logo* Teacher Tutorial.

Spatial Sense and Geometry with Geo-Logo

How do explorations with *Geo-Logo* help students become more competent in geometric thinking? *Geo-Logo* is a special geometry-oriented version of Logo, a well-known computer language used internationally in teaching mathematics.

In *Geo-Logo*, the emphasis is on constructing geometric paths, figures, and designs, rather than on recognizing and naming them. *Geo-Logo* provides an environment in which students can easily create and modify geometric figures using mathematical language. This language includes the *measurement* of the parts of the figures, or paths, that they draw. For example, to draw a square, students must give commands that specify the lengths of the sides and the amount of turn at the corners.

Geo-Logo requires students to communicate with the turtle in a geometry-oriented language. In the process of making squares, students see that the sides must be equal lengths because all four commands that draw sides have the same length in them. They know that the corners are equal because they must tell the turtle to turn the same amount at each corner.

Student-created *Geo-Logo* programs can be run repeatedly, reproducing the same drawing each time (assuming the turtle starts in the same place). Students can actually study what their programs do by running them one step at a time and fixing individual pieces of them.

Finally, computers in general, and *Geo-Logo* in particular, are motivating to many students. The artistic aspect of some of the activities, such as Shapes and Pictures, can provide an engaging, constructive approach to geometric concepts.

About Choice Time

Choice Time is an opportunity for students to work on a variety of activities that focus on similar mathematical content. Choice Time activities are found in most units of the grade 2 *Investigations* curriculum. These generally alternate with whole-class activities in which students work individually or in pairs on one or two problems. Each format offers somewhat different classroom experiences. Both are important for students to be engaged in.

In Choice Time the activities are not sequential. As students move among them, they continually revisit some of the important concepts and ideas they are learning. Many activities are designed with the intent that students will work on them more than once. By playing a game a second or third time or solving similar problems, students refine strategies, see a variety of approaches, and bring new knowledge to familiar experiences.

You may want to limit the number of students who work on a Choice Time activity at one time.

Often when a new choice is introduced, many students want to do it first. Assure them that they will be able to try each choice. In many cases, the quantity of materials available limits the number of students who can do an activity at a time. Even if this is not the case, set guidelines about the number of students who work on each choice. This gives students the opportunity to work in smaller groups and to make decisions about what they want and need to do. It also provides a chance to return and do some choices more than once.

Initially, you may need to help students plan what they do. Rather than organizing them into groups and circulating the groups every 15 minutes, support students in making decisions about the choices they do. Making choices, planning their time, and taking responsibility for their own learning are important aspects of a student's school experience. If some students return to the

Continued on next page

same activity over and over again without trying others, suggest that they make a different first choice and then choose the favorite activity as a second choice.

How to Set Up Choices

Some teachers prefer to have choices set up at centers or stations around the room. At each center, students will find the materials needed to complete the activity. Other teachers prefer to store materials in a central location and have students bring materials to their desks or tables. In either case, materials should be readily accessible to students, and students should be expected to take responsibility for cleaning up and returning materials to their appropriate storage locations. Giving students a "5 minutes until cleanup" warning before the end of an activity session allows them to finish what they are working on and prepare for the transition.

You may find that you need to experiment with a few different structures before finding a setup that works best.

The Role of the Student

Establish clear guidelines when you introduce Choice Time activities. Discuss students' responsibilities:

- Try every choice at least once.
- Work with a partner or alone. (Some activities require that students work in pairs, while others can be done either alone or with partners.)
- Keep track, on paper, of the choices you have worked on.
- Keep all your work in your math folder.
- Ask questions of other students when you don't understand or feel stuck. (Some teachers establish the rule, "Ask two other students before me," requiring students to check with two peers before coming to the teacher for help.)

Students can use their Weekly Logs to keep track of their work. As students finish a choice, they write it on their log and place any work they have done in their folder. Some teachers list the choices for sessions on a chart, the board, or the overhead projector to help students keep track of what they need to do.

In any classroom there will be a range of how much work students complete. Some choices include extensions and additional problems for students to do when they have completed their required work. Encourage students to return to choices they have done before, do another problem or two from the choice, or play a game again.

At the end of a Choice Time session, spend a few minutes discussing with students what went smoothly, what sorts of issues arose and how they were resolved, and what students enjoyed or found difficult. Encourage students to be involved in the process of finding solutions to problems that come up in the classroom. In doing so, they take responsibility for their own behavior and become involved with establishing classroom policies. You may want to make the choices available at other times during the day.

The Role of the Teacher

Choice Time provides you with the opportunity to observe and listen to students while they work. At times, you may want to meet with individual students, pairs, or small groups who need help or whom you haven't had a chance to observe before, or to do individual assessments. Recording your observations of students will help you keep track of how they are interacting with materials and solving problems. The **Teacher Note,** Keeping Track of Students' Work (p. 25), offers some strategies for recording and using your observations.

During the initial weeks of Choice Time, most of your time probably will be spent circulating around the classroom, helping students get settled into activities, and monitoring the overall management of the classroom. Once routines are familiar and well established, students will become more independent and responsible for their work. This will allow you to spend more concentrated periods of time observing the class as a whole or working with individuals and small groups.

Keeping Track of Students' Work

Throughout the *Investigations* curriculum there are numerous opportunities to observe students as they work. Teacher observations are an important part of ongoing assessment. While individual observations are snapshots of a student's experience with a single activity, when considered over time they can provide an informative and detailed picture. These observations can be useful in documenting and assessing a student's growth. They offer important information when preparing for family conferences or writing student reports.

Your observations of students will vary throughout the unit. At times you may be interested in particular strategies that students are developing to solve problems. Or you might want to observe how students use or do not use materials to help them solve problems. At other times you may be interested in noting the strategy that a student uses when playing a game during Choice Time. Class discussions also provide many opportunities to take note of students' ideas and thinking.

Keeping observation notes on a class of 28 students can become overwhelming and time-consuming. You will probably find it necessary to develop some sort of system to record and keep track of your observations of students. A few ideas and suggestions are offered here, but you will want to find a system that works for you.

A class list of names is a convenient way of jotting down observations of students. Since the space is limited, it is not possible to write lengthy notes. However, when kept over time these short observations provide important information.

Stick-on address labels can be kept on clipboards around the room. Notes can be taken on individual students and then these labels can be peeled off and stuck into a file that you set up for each student.

Alternatively, jotting down brief notes at the end of each week may work well for you. Some teachers find that this is a useful way of reflecting on the class as a whole, on the curriculum, and on individual students. Planning for the next weeks' activities often develops from these weekly reflections.

In addition to your own notes on students, all students will keep a folder of work. This work and the daily entries on the Weekly Logs can document a student's experience. Together they can help you keep track of the students in your classroom, assess their growth over time, and communicate this information to others. At the end of each unit there is a list of things you might choose to keep in students' folders.

D I A L O G U E   B O X

Matching Lengths

In a discussion following the activity Scavenger Hunt 1 (p. 20), these students are sharing their strategies for comparing lengths. They describe and demonstrate the ways they used direct comparison, indirect comparison, and nonstandard units.

Let's share some of the ways you are finding things in the classroom that are as long as our paper strips. What did you use to help you compare lengths?

Bjorn: We used cubes. The first strip is as long as 27 cubes.

Did anyone else use cubes? How did the cubes work? Naomi?

Naomi: The cubes worked OK, but sometimes they weren't exactly the right length, but between. That made it harder. And sometimes, if you had to use a lot of cubes, it was hard. The cubes broke apart.

It sounds like when you used cubes you could tell if something was *about* the same length as a paper strip. *About* the same length is fine. It doesn't have to be exact.

Naomi's experience with the cubes makes me think that cubes might be hard to use when the paper strip is long, like Strip B [*name a long strip in your classroom*]. What other measuring tool could you use to help you compare a long paper strip to an object?

Rosie: We used string.

How did that work? Did you put the string next to the strip?

Rosie: On top of it. And then Tim cut it. And then we compared it to things, and we found out that the blue table is the same length as B.

Did anyone else use other ways? Graham?

Graham: For the shortest strip, D, I used my knuckle. It was 16 knuckles long. Then for the strip in the middle, I measured with my hands and I got 8.

Can you show us how you measured Strip C with your hands, Graham?

Graham demonstrates alternately placing his left and right hands, heel to fingertip, along the paper strip, counting as he does so: 1, 2, 3, 4, 5, 6, 7, 8.

Graham used two different ways to compare strips. Did other people use more than one way? [*Several hands go up.*] Carla?

Carla: Well, D is pretty short, so we just held things up next to it. And B is very long, so we held a paper strip up to it and cut it the same length. Then we compared that to things in the room.

Using Related Units of Measure

In Scavenger Hunt 2, students find items that are a certain number of nonstandard units long, then predict and measure the length of the items when a second, related nonstandard unit is used. The units the students use, blue strips and yellow strips, are in a 2-to-1 relationship.

During a Choice Time session (p. 17), two students are searching for something that is 5 blue strips long. The teacher notices Simon lay 5 strips along the edge of a bookshelf with gaps between the strips.

What have you found?

Simon: This bookshelf is 5 blue strips long.

Does it matter that there is space between the end of the strips?

Harris: Yeah, you've got to push them together, Simon.

Simon: But then they won't fit. The shelf is longer.

The teacher lays 5 more blue strips on a nearby table, end-to-end.

Are the bookshelf and this table the same length? Are they both 5 strips long?

Simon: No, the bookshelf is longer than the table. The table is 5 strips long.

[*Simon writes "table" on his student sheet and looks at the next question, "What is 4 blue strips long?" He lays 4 strips end to end on the table, looks around the room, and then decides it would be easier to measure with a piece of string. He cuts a string the length of 4 units, then walks around the room looking for something to match its length.*]

In a later session, the teacher discusses the activity with the class. Now the conversation focuses on the 2-to-1 relationship.

If you had already measured something with blue strips, how did you predict how many yellow strips it was going to be?

Juanita: I thought of how you go 2, 4, 6, 8, 10, and I went like that because 2 yellows would fill in 1 blue.

Juanita counted the blue strips by 2's to make her prediction. Did anyone predict another way?

Lila: I doubled the number of blue strips.

Why?

Lila: Because 2 yellow strips makes 1 blue strip. It takes 2 yellow for every blue strip.

So Lila doubled the number of blue strips. When I put a blue strip next to a yellow strip, like this [*places strips side by side*], you can see that the blue strip is twice as long as the yellow strip.

Remember what we measured with 3 blue strips?

Lionel: My desk.

Which way?

Lionel: This way. [*He gestures to indicate width.*]

Right, the width. So how many yellow?

Lionel: 6.

Choices About Measurement

Materials

- Adding machine tape (4–6 rolls)
- Interlocking cubes (about 30 per student)
- Masking tape (2–4 rolls)
- Scissors
- Game or place markers
- Blue and yellow paper strips (from Sessions 2–4)
- Computers with *Geo-Logo* installed
- Projection device or large-screen monitor
- Prepared measurement riddles
- Student Sheet 8 (1 per student)
- Student Sheet 9 (1 per student, homework)
- Student Sheet 10 (1 per student, homework)
- Student Sheet 7 (as needed, homework)
- Chart paper

What Happens

Students are introduced to three additional choices. In How Far Can You Jump? and Measurement Riddles they measure and compare lengths. In Giant Steps, a computer activity, they move a "turtle" by different-sized unit lengths. Scavenger Hunt 2: How Many Paper Strips?, is another choice for these sessions. A class discussion at the end of Session 7 gives students the opportunity to talk about and reflect on their work. Their work focuses on:

- iterating units
- seeing that units can be related, and that when you know how long something is in one unit, you can figure out its length in a related unit
- using units to find the difference between two lengths; that is, how much longer one length is than another

Start-Up

Today's Number

- **Calendar Date** If you are using the calendar date for Today's Number, brainstorm with students ways to express the number. Suggest students use combinations of 10 in their number sentences. For example, if today's number is 23 and one number sentence is 10 + 10 + 3, ask students if there is another way of making 10, such as (6 + 4)+ (6 + 4) + 3, or (4 + 3 + 2 + 1) + (4 + 3 + 2 + 1) + 3. Record their expressions on chart paper.

- **Number of School Days** If you are using the number of school days for Today's Number, and the number is over 100, focus on ways to make 100 using both addition and subtraction. For example, if the number is 134, solutions could be 200 – 100 + 34, or 150 – 50 + 34. Add a card to the class counting strip and fill in another number on the 200 chart.

Activity

How Far Can You Jump?

Today we have two new activities you can choose during Choice Time. How Far Can You Jump? is one of the activities.

Show students the areas you have set up for this activity and the materials they will be using. (Set this activity up in two or more areas, with each area providing enough space for students to jump.) Depending on both the space available and your supply of interlocking cubes (a frog jump may measure

40 cubes), you may need to limit to two pairs the number of students working in each jumping area.

To do this activity, you and your partner take turns jumping from the starting line on the floor. You each make three different jumps: a regular kid-style jump, a frog jump, and a rabbit hop.

Ask students to imagine a frog, the shape of its body, and what it looks like when it jumps. When students do a frog jump, they jump from a squatting position, starting and ending with both hands and feet on the floor. In a similar way, introduce the rabbit hop, which is done from almost a standing position, with knees bent and feet together. As for the kid-style jump, ask students to describe how they usually jump forward, how they stand, and whether their feet are together or apart. Bring students to an agreement about what a kid-style jump should be for this activity.

Although this activity is noncompetitive, it's helpful to come to a consensus about how to jump from the starting line. Some possibilities are: toes on the line or just behind it; heels on the line; or just standing on the line. You should also agree what to measure; for example, from the back of the heel or from the starting line, to the tip of the toes at the end of the jump.

Each time you jump, mark your stopping point. Your partner will help you cut a strip of adding machine tape the same length as your jump. What are some ways to mark where your jump ends?

Students might suggest having a partner put a cube down where they land, or marking their end points with masking tape. Have two students demonstrate how to cut the adding machine tape to show the length of the jump. One student jumps and marks where the jump ended. Then the partner tapes one end of the adding machine tape on the starting point, unrolls it to the endpoint, and cuts it. Suggest that students write on the adding machine tape which jump it represents and their name.

Note: If a student in your class can't jump, he or she can be the official referee, making sure that toes don't creep over the starting line and having the final say over disputes about length of jumps.

When you have finished your three jumps, use cubes to measure the paper strips. Find your longest jump and your shortest jump. Then figure out how many cubes longer your longest jump is than your shortest jump.

Provide each student with Student Sheet 8, How Far Can You Jump? Ask students to record their jump measurements on their paper strips, then solve the problem on the student sheet. It's important that they write about their strategies for solving this problem. Tell students that they will have the opportunity to continue this activity during Choice Time.

❖ **Tip for the Linguistically Diverse Classroom** Draw students' attention to the pictures of the frog jump, the rabbit hop and the kid jump on the top of Student Sheet 8. Suggest that students add a small drawing next to the words *frog*, *rabbit*, *kid*, and *cubes* as a visual reminder. It may also help students if they draw a long line near the word *longest* and a short line near the word *shortest*.

If students have used the grade 2 *Investigations* unit *Putting Together and Taking Apart*, they will have had experiences with comparison problems such as this one, in which they find the difference between two quantities (or, in this case, two measures of length). Remind students to solve the problem in a way that makes sense to them, to use numbers and words or pictures to explain how they solved it, and to use a different strategy to check their work. See the **Teacher Note**, Combining, Comparing, and Measuring (p. 41), for strategies students used in one classroom.

Introduce students to this choice by solving a measurement riddle to-gether. (Refer to p. 4, Other Preparation, for information on preparing Measurement Riddles.) Read aloud the riddle given here, adapting it to fit the calendar (or another object) in your classroom. Or use a riddle you have created. You might want to write the riddle on the chalkboard.

I'm a rectangle and I hang on the wall.

I'm 48 cubes wide and 32 cubes tall.

What could I be?

Solve the riddle together. Then explain that solving measurement riddles has been added to Choice Time. Post the riddles you have written on chart paper.

Introduce Giant Steps to the class using a computer and a projection device for screen display. If a projection device is not available, use the largest available monitor or show the game to smaller groups of students. Review how to open *Geo-Logo,* then choose Giant Steps. (Work through the Giant Steps activity in the *Geo-Logo* Teacher Tutorial p. 102 before working on the computer with students.)

Read the directions, then click on **[OK]** or press **<return>**. Two turtles, each facing a target object the same distance away, appear.

Explain that just as in the Steps game, the goal is to get the turtle to the tar-get with the fewest possible commands. But in Giant Steps one turtle has a step that is double or triple the other's. This relationship is indicated by the number next to the larger unit.

Click on the turtle whose unit length is 1. Have students suggest a forward command for this turtle. Then click on the other turtle. Challenge students to use the measure from the first command to figure out an estimate for the other turtle.

After you have demonstrated how to use Giant Steps, tell students that this will be one of the activities they can choose during Choice Time.

Choice Time

Add How Far Can You Jump?, Measurement Riddles, and Giant Steps to the list of choices on the board. If students have completed Scavenger Hunt 1 and everyone has tried the Steps activity, you may want to cross these off the list. (If necessary, refer to previous Choice Time activities (p. 16) for materials and set-up information and suggestions on what to watch for as you observe students for the first three activities on the list.)

```
1. Scavenger Hunt 1

2. Scavenger Hunt 2

3. Steps (computer)

4. How Far Can You Jump?

5. Measurement Riddles

6. Giant Steps (computer)
```

Explain to students that for today and the next two sessions, they will be finishing Scavenger Hunt 2 and working on two new measurement activities. Plan to have a discussion about Scavenger Hunt 2 at the beginning of Session 7.

Choice 4: How Far Can You Jump?

Materials: Adding machine tape; masking tape; scissors; cubes or counters; Student Sheet 8, How Far Can You Jump?

Students work in pairs. Taking turns, each student takes three jumps from the starting line: one kid-style jump, one frog jump, and one rabbit hop. One student jumps and marks where the jump ended, using a cube or counter as a marker, or using masking tape and labeling it with his or her name. A partner cuts a length of adding machine tape that extends from the starting line to the point where the jump ends.

After both partners have paper strips for their jumps, each student identifies his or her longest and shortest jumps. Students measure the adding machine tapes in cubes and record the measurements. They use this information to find the distance in cubes between their longest and shortest jump, recording the measure on the student sheet.

Choice 5: Measurement Riddles

Materials: Interlocking cubes, Measurement Riddles (posted or on teacher-made student sheet)

Students find possible solutions for Measurement Riddles you have created. Keeping in mind the clues in the riddle, they measure to find classroom items that are possible solutions. More than one solution may be possible.

Extension: Students can measure objects and write their own riddles.

Choice 6: Giant Steps

Materials: Computers with *Geo-Logo* installed

Students take turns entering commands to make the turtles move forward. The goal is to get both turtles to the target using the fewest commands.

Observing the Students

Use the following questions as a guide for observing students at work. For observations suggestions for the first three activities on the list, refer to p. 18.

How Far Can You Jump?

- How do students measure their jumps with interlocking cubes? (Some students might join cubes one by one, counting by 1's as they go or after the distance is covered. Other students might use groups of 10 [or 5] to count the cubes representing the distance.)

- How do students find the difference between their longest and shortest jumps? (Some students might compare the cube trains for the two jumps and simply count how many cubes longer one is than the other. Others might use an addition strategy, such as counting up from the smaller number to the larger. Depending on the numbers used, they might count on by 1's or by 10's and keep track of the amount added on with tallies, their fingers, or with numbers. Or some students might subtract the smaller number from the larger number.)

Measurement Riddles

- How do students measure the dimensions the riddles describe?
- Do they see that some riddles may have multiple solutions?

Giant Steps

- How do students estimate how many steps forward a turtle should take?
- Do students use their partner's or their own path to estimate how far their turtle should go?
- Do they take into account the length of their partner's unit? If so, how?

Discuss how to adjust for different unit lengths. Ask if it makes sense, for example, for turtle1 to cover a distance in 12 steps, with a unit three times as long as that of turtle2, which covered the same distance in only 4 steps. While students are working, encourage them to discuss and improve their strategies for estimating distances.

At the end of each session, after students have cleaned up their materials, remind them to record what they have done on their Weekly Logs.

Class Discussion: Scavenger Hunt 2—How Many Paper Strips?

Once all students have completed Scavenger Hunt 2 (probably at the beginning of Session 7), have a brief discussion about using the blue and yellow strips. Having this conversation before students complete Choice Time gives them an opportunity to try new measuring strategies when they finish the Scavenger Hunt. Have some strips handy for this discussion.

Have students share some of their results for the blue strips and their predictions and actual results for the yellow strips. Then focus the discussion on the relationship between the blue and yellow strips.

I'm interested in how you predicted how many yellow strips long things were. When you found something that was 6 blue strips long, how did you predict how many yellow strips long it would be? Did you notice anything about the blue and yellow strips that helped you predict?

Some students may have discovered that for each object the number of yellow strips is twice the number of blue strips. Ask them why this is so. Students may respond "it's a pattern" or "it's doubles." To encourage them to think about why this pattern works, line up one yellow strip next to the blue strip so that students can visualize how a second yellow strip would fit. Have a student place the second yellow strip next to the first one so that others can see that two yellow strips are equal in length to one blue strip. Ask a volunteer to describe this relationship.

Ask students to explain how they measured with the strips. Discrepancies in measurements may come up during this discussion. If so, you might use this as an opportunity to compare ways of measuring. Or you might offer your own example for discussion:

yellow strip

blue strip

I noticed that some people measured this book and found that it was 4 yellow strips long. When another student measured the same book, he used 3 yellow strips and part of another one. How do you think this book could have two different measurements?

Talk about some different ways these hypothetical students might have measured, for example, lining up strips end to end or leaving gaps between strips when lining them up. Do students see that one method is more accurate than the other?

Ask students to share some of the ways they measured items that were more than 5 blue strips long. Students may have used strategies such as removing strips used in the beginning of the measuring and reusing them; flipping a strip over its end; and carefully placing one unit over and over again. All of these strategies require keeping track of how many times a unit is used.

By the end of Session 7, you may want to give students an opportunity to share their work on How Far Can You Jump? and Measurement Riddles.

Students may have used a variety of strategies to measure their shortest and longest jumps and find the difference between them in How Far Can You Jump? For example, some students may have measured each jump with interlocking cubes and compared the cube trains to find the difference. Others may have recorded the lengths in cubes and found the difference between the two numbers representing the measurements. Another possibility is to line up the shortest and longest strips side by side, measure the shortest jump, then measure the additional length (the difference) on the longest strip. The length of the longest jump is found by adding the two parts together.

Class Discussion: Choice Time Activities

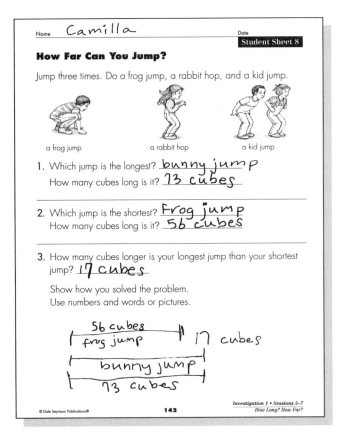

Name Camilla

Date

Student Sheet 8

How Far Can You Jump?

Jump three times. Do a frog jump, a rabbit hop, and a kid jump.

a frog jump   a rabbit hop   a kid jump

1. Which jump is the longest? bunny jump
   How many cubes long is it? 73 cubes

2. Which jump is the shortest? Frog jump
   How many cubes long is it? 56 cubes

3. How many cubes longer is your longest jump than your shortest jump? 17 cubes

   Show how you solved the problem.
   Use numbers and words or pictures.

   56 cubes frog jump   17 cubes
   bunny jump   73 cubes

© Dale Seymour Publications®   142   Investigation 1 • Sessions 5–7
How Long? How Far?

Students can also share their solutions to the Measurement Riddles. If they have written their own riddles as well, these can be posted for others to solve.

Laura

I am round and on the floor.
You put things in me.
I am 32 cubs tall.

What could I be ?

Paul

I am on a table,
I am 23 cubs long and
I am eigteet cudes wide
who am I?

I am on a desk
I am ninefen cube widt,
and I am 12 cubes long.

Note: Collect the blue and yellow paper strips, as students will be using these again in Session 8.

Sessions 5, 6, and 7 Follow-Up

 **Homework**

Measuring at Home   After Session 5, students use the measuring strips they cut out earlier in the unit to measure familiar objects at home. They record their work on Student Sheet 9, Measuring at Home. Have a few extra copies of Student Sheet 7, Measuring Strips, available for students who may need another copy.

Measurement Riddles   After Session 7, students write a measurement riddle on Student Sheet 10 for someone at home to solve. They might write their riddle about an object they measured for homework after Session 5 (on Student Sheet 9), or they might measure a new object and write their riddle about it.

 **Extension**

Using Related Units   To encourage students to think about halves of quantities, have them measure other items in the classroom using the yellow strip first. After finding out how many yellow strips long or wide an object is, they predict how many blue strips long it will be and then measure.

Measuring Our Classroom

What Happens

As an assessment, students use units of their own choosing to measure the width of the classroom. As a class, they discuss the variety of measures they found. Their work focuses on:

- iterating units
- thinking about the need for a standard unit

Start-Up

Today's Number

Calendar Date *and* Number of School Days   Students can express today's number using coins (pennies, nickels, dimes, quarters). For example, if the number is 28 (calendar date) possible combinations are: 25¢ + 1¢ + 1¢ + 1¢ or 10¢ + 10¢ + 5¢ + 1¢ + 1¢ + 1¢. If Today's Number is over 100, such as 137, a possible combination is 25¢ + 25¢ + 25¢ + 25¢ + 25¢ + 10¢ + 1¢ + 1¢. If you are counting the number of school days, add a card to the class counting strip and fill in another number on the blank 200 chart.

Materials

- Interlocking cubes (about 30 per student)
- Blue and yellow paper strips (from Sessions 2, 3, and 4)
- Other nonstandard measuring units such as craft sticks
- Chart paper

Activity

Assessment

Measuring Our Classroom

Choose one dimension of your classroom (length or width) for students to measure. Since students may choose small units of measure and require a large number of units, you may want to have them measure the smaller dimension of the room.

Because the terms *how wide* or *width* may not be familiar to some students, point out the width of the classroom as you introduce this activity.

Since we have been working with measuring, I've been wondering about how wide our classroom is. Can you think of a reason why we might need to know the width of our classroom?

Today, you'll be working with partners to measure the width of the classroom. You and your partner will need to agree on what you will use to measure with. You can use the blue paper strips or the yellow paper strips. Or you might want to use cubes, or paper clips, or craft sticks [*or other nonstandard units*]. You will also need to decide *how* you will use your tools to figure out how wide our classroom is.

Ask students to share some of the ways they could measure this distance. As they suggest materials they might use, encourage them to describe and perhaps demonstrate how they would use them. For example, students might line up units end to end, or show how they could iterate a larger unit, such as a train of 10 cubes. Be sure also to focus on ways to count a large quantity of units and on how to keep track of how many units are used or how many times a unit is iterated.

Suppose you are using cubes to measure the width of the classroom. That would probably take a lot of cubes. How can you count all the cubes you use?

Students will probably suggest counting by 5's or 10's and may suggest breaking the cubes into trains 5 or 10 cubes long to do so. Ask students how they might do this. Would they count from 1 to 10 to make each train of 10, and then count all the trains by 10's? Would they break off a train of 10 and use it as a measuring unit to make more trains of 10, then count the trains by 10's?

Counting all the cubes you use seems like it would take a long time. Can you think of ways to keep track of how many cubes you use while you make a train going across the classroom?

Let pairs or small groups of students discuss this problem. Then, together, brainstorm a few ways to keep track of cubes used while building the train. Students might suggest that one student count or tally cubes while the other builds, or use a particular color cube for every tenth cube. You might also talk about how these strategies could work for other nonstandard units—for instance, marking every tenth paper strip or craft stick, or perhaps linking paper clips in tens.

If any students have suggested iterating a single, larger unit, ask them to think about and discuss how to know where to place the unit each time and how to keep track of the number of units used. See the **Teacher Note,** Combining, Comparing, and Measuring (p. 41), for strategies students used in one classroom.

Pair the students and have them decide which materials they will use to measure with. Explain that after they measure, they should record their findings on paper and write about or draw how they measured. When they are ready, partners should get materials and go to the area of the room where they will begin working.

Observing the Students Observe how students are measuring, counting, and keeping track of how many units they have used. You may need to offer some guidance in choosing units to measure with. As you circulate, try to get to every student, especially students you have had less opportunity to observe and talk with about their thinking.

- Are students joining cubes one by one? If students are lining up paper strips (or other nonstandard units), how are they placing the strips? Do they line up the strips end to end? Or are they leaving gaps between strips or overlapping them?

- If students are iterating a single unit, such as a train of 10 cubes, note how they are placing the unit each time. Are they flipping the unit end over end? Are they placing a finger or marker at the end of the unit, then picking it up and placing it so that the starting end of the unit is at that point? How are students keeping track of how many times they have iterated the unit? For instance, does one student count or tally each time the partner iterates the unit?

- Are students using a strategy that enables them to keep track of how many units they have used? For instance, do they mark or indicate every tenth unit in some way (for example, using a different-color cube, marking a paper strip or craft stick)?

- How are students counting cubes or other small units? Do some students want to count only by 1's? Do some students lose track of their count? If you observe students having difficulty keeping track or counting large quantities of small units, encourage them to choose a larger unit. Other students may need to be reminded to move the cubes they have counted away from those they have not. To encourage students who rely on counting by 1's to use grouping strategies, suggest that they double-check their count by counting again in a different way.

Class Discussion: Measuring Our Classroom

Ask students to share the measurements they found for the width of the classroom. As they do so, ask questions to encourage thinking about the differences in results and the differences among the units.

Imani and Carla said they used 60 craft sticks. Who else used craft sticks? How many did you use?

Most students who used craft sticks found that our room is about 60 craft sticks wide. Simon and Rosie used the blue paper strips. Do you think they used more or fewer than 60? A lot fewer or a little fewer? [*Hold a craft stick and a blue paper strip side by side so students can compare the two units.*] **Why?**

Continue with several other comparisons and predictions, such as cubes and paper clips, yellow strips and blue strips, and craft sticks and cubes. As students share actual results, record on chart paper their measurements along with the units used (for example, 48 blue strips). Because the inverse relationship between the size and number of units needed takes time to construct, these predictions may be challenging or even difficult for some students.

It's interesting that when we measured the width of our classroom, we got so many different measurements. How do you suppose we could have all these different measurements?

Students may have a number of interesting ideas about how this could happen: they measured parts of the room having different widths, perhaps narrower due to shelves or a closet; they measured in different ways; they made mistakes. However, after comparing several different units, some students may conclude that because they used different materials to measure with, they got different measurements for the width of the classroom. Focus for a few minutes on this concept.

Paul is saying that because we used units that are different sizes, we got different measurements. Let's compare some of the measurement units we used. Linda and Tim used the yellow strips, and Simon and Rosie used the blue strips. How do their measurements compare? How do their measuring units compare?

Some students will see that the larger the unit, the smaller the measurement. You may want to encourage their thinking about relationship between size and number of units by measuring a short length such as a desktop in a large unit and a small unit, being sure to place the two rows of units side by side. Since students are familiar with the blue and yellow strips, you might begin with those units, followed by a less familiar comparison, for example, craft sticks and yellow strips. As you discuss your example, point out that the length measured stays the same; that is, the desktop is not longer when it is measured in smaller units. Encourage students to describe that more yellow strips than craft sticks are needed to cover the length of the desktop because the yellow strips are smaller. Since craft sticks are longer than the yellow strips, fewer sticks are needed to cover the same distance.

Combining, Comparing, and Measuring

As students find and compare lengths, they draw on their knowledge of number. For instance, students use their understanding of number relationships when they measure an object using strips of one length, then predict its measurement in strips of a related length, and when they discuss the various measurements that result when different units are used.

Students also apply their knowledge of number and of combining and comparing numbers as they solve problems about measurement. How Far Can You Jump? and Measuring Our Classroom are two measurement activities that lend themselves to students' use of number relationships and strategies for combining and comparing numbers. In How Far Can You Jump? some students may use counting on to find the difference between their longest and shortest jumps. In the student's work that follows, Helena shows how she used counting on to find the difference between her frog jump (36 cubes) and

her rabbit hop (18 cubes). Note that she counts each number counted on by writing a smaller number above it.

Other students, however, break apart and combine numbers, as Graham's work illustrates:

Name __Graham__   Date
Student Sheet 8

How Far Can You Jump?

Jump three times. Do a frog jump, a rabbit hop, and a kid jump.

a frog jump   a rabbit hop   a kid jump

1. Which jump is the longest? __Person Jump__
   How many cubes long is it? __94__

2. Which jump is the shortest? __frog Jump__
   How many cubes long is it? __61__

3. How many cubes longer is your longest jump than your shortest jump? __3 3__

   Show how you solved the problem.
   Use numbers and words or pictures.

   $$90-60=30$$
   $$4-1=3$$
   $$30+3=33$$ $$33$$

© Dale Seymour Publications®   142   *Investigation 1 • Sessions 5–7*
How Long? How Far?

Name __Helena__   Date
Student Sheet 8

How Far Can You Jump?

Jump three times. Do a frog jump, a rabbit hop, and a kid jump.

a frog jump   a rabbit hop   a kid jump

1. Which jump is the longest? __Frog Jump__
   How many cubes long is it? __36__

2. Which jump is the shortest? __Rabbit__
   How many cubes long is it? __18__

3. How many cubes longer is your longest jump than your shortest jump? __(18)__

   Show how you solved the problem.
   Use numbers and words or pictures.

   I counted on
   18) 19 20 21 22 23 24 25 26 27
   28 29 30 31 32 33 34 35 36

© Dale Seymour Publications®   142   *Investigation 1 • Sessions 5–7*
How Long? How Far?

Students also use a range of strategies in Measuring Our Classroom, the assessment activity that ends Investigation 1. Although a few students may continue to count units one by one, most students use more efficient and sophisticated measurement strategies.

■ After extending the units across the classroom, some students group them into 10's and then count. If the units are small in size, students might also make and count groups of 100.

■ Some students iterate units. In one classroom, several students arrived at iterating 10 cubes, or the length of 10 of some other unit, as a

Continued on next page

strategy for finding the width of the classroom. One student described the process this way: ". . . you use 10 cubes and then just do 10 and put your finger to show where you stop, then 20, 30, 40. . . ." Students might also use a combination of repeatedly placing units end to end and iterating units, particularly when there are not enough units to cover the entire distance across the classroom.

Karina and Paul describe their strategy of joining 10's to make 100, then iterating a train of 100 cubes.

Karina: Well, we took 9 cubes and then we put a black cube after the ninth cube. Then we counted by 10's up to 100.

Paul: Once we got to 100 cubes, we took a yellow strip and put it under the last cube so the end of the yellow strip lined up with the end of the last cube. So we took 100 cubes and pushed them over so the first cube we ever made lined up with the strip, and did that over and over.

Iteration strategies require keeping track of how many times the unit is placed to arrive at the total number of units used. When students do not have enough units and iterate a group of units, they keep track of and combine the groups of units to find the total number of units used. To solve this real problem, students draw on their experience with combining numbers.

Juanita   Linda

64 lihK   64 link   64 link
                 some xtras

$64 + 64 = 128$

$128 + 64 = 192$

$64 - 5 = 59$

$192 + 59 = 251$

Juanita and Linda used 64 links as their unit but had to subtract 5 links because the last section of the room would not take a whole string of 64.

Lila

Tim

$54 + 54 + 54 + 54 + 24 =$
  100 8   100   8

$100 + 100 = 200$
$8 + 8 = 16$

$200 + 16 = 216$

$216 + 24$
200 30 10

$200 + 30 + 10 = 240$

Lila and Tim iterated a group of 54 units; again, at the end, only part of the group would fit. After recording the groups of units used, the students combined them in ways they found meaningful.

How Wide Is Our Classroom?

Measurement, like counting, answers the question "How many?" Unlike counting a group of objects, however, measurement involves breaking a continuous attribute such as length into discrete, countable, equal units. When we ask "How wide is our classroom?" we mean "How many units equal the width of our classroom?" The number of units required depends on the size of the units used.

During a class discussion (p. 39), students share results, then make conjectures about discrepancies in measurements. They consider how the units were placed.

Let's take a look at some of the results we listed. It's interesting that three pairs of students who measured the width of the room using blue strips, used about 40 strips. [*Teacher points to 40, 40½, and 41 on the chart paper.*] But another pair used 52 blue strips, and one pair used 33. How could they have gotten these different measurements using the blue strips?

Naomi: Maybe some kids measured across a different part of the room.

Are different parts of the room different sizes?

Naomi: Well, you could measure just to the shelves, not all the way to the window.

Lionel: If you didn't measure straight across, you would use more strips.

Say a little more about that, Lionel.

Lionel: Well, if you made a turn, or you went around a desk, you would use up more strips. That could be how 52 strips got used.

So some students might not have measured the same distance across the room. Or maybe they did not make a straight path. Do you think it matters how you line up the paper strips? If I measure a desktop like this [*overlaps 8 strips*] instead of like this [*places 5 strips end to end*], would that change how many strips are used?

Linda: You use more strips when you put them on top of each other like that.

What if I did it like this? [*Measures the desktop with just 4 strips, leaving gaps between strips.*]

Lila: But you didn't cover the whole thing.

The conversation includes other ways to measure.

So far, we've talked about how to line up units across the room. Did anyone measure a different way? Ayaz?

Ayaz: We put 10 cubes together, and we just kept doing 10.

How did you do 10's? Can you show us what you and Jeffrey did?

Ayaz: We put 10 down like this. Then I put my finger here, and moved the 10 to here.

Jeffrey: I made an X each time we did that. Then we counted the X's by 10's.

So your strategy helped you to keep track of how many cubes you used, too.

Later the teacher focuses on why different measurements were obtained. Most students can see that because units of different sizes were used, the measurements are different. A few students refer to the inverse relationship between the size and number of units used.

Let's look at our results. We got different measurements for the width of the classroom. Sixty craft sticks, 40 blue strips, about 80 yellow strips, and more than 300 cubes! How could we have all these different measurements?

Juanita: We used different things to measure.

Jess: Some people used cubes and some used other things.

Paul: Yeah, but the things we measured with were different sizes. Like the craft sticks are pretty big, and cubes are small.

Why is the size of the things you measure with important? Any ideas?

Paul: Because if you measure with a tiny thing, you need to use a lot of them.

Paths and *Geo-Logo*

What Happens

Session 1: Walking, Visualizing, and Representing Paths   Students walk paths in their classroom and describe their movements. After walking a path in the gym or on the playground, they record their paths, and then follow their representations and describe their movements.

Sessions 2 and 3: Investigating Turns   Students turn their bodies and describe how many units they have turned. They use a Turtle Turner to help them estimate and measure turtle turns and are introduced to Maze, a computer activity in which students move the *Geo-Logo* turtle along a path.

Sessions 4 and 5: Measuring Paths   Students use paper strips to construct and then compare two paths between the same places—one path is straight, and the other path has turns. They describe where their paths go and how long each path is. This activity is used as a Teacher Checkpoint.

Sessions 6, 7, and 8: Moving on a Grid   Students compare lengths of paths represented on grid paper. They then plan and draw their own paths on grid paper and determine the length of the paths. A computer activity also provides students with experience with paths on grids.

Ongoing Excursion: *Geo-Logo:* Shapes and Pictures   Students are introduced to Shapes and Pictures, an on-going activity in which they use *Geo-Logo*'s tools and commands to make shapes and pictures of their own design.

Mathematical Emphasis

- Moving along a path
- Visualizing and then representing a path
- Determining path length by iterating and counting units
- Comparing lengths of paths by comparing the number of units used to measure each path

What to Plan Ahead of Time

Materials

- Drawing paper (Session 1)
- Crayons, markers (Session 1)
- Sidewalk chalk (Session 1, optional)
- Clipboards: 1 per pair (Session 1, optional)
- Adding machine tape: 6 to 8 rolls (Session 1)
- Carpet remnants, traffic cones, or large geometric shapes cut from poster board (Session 1)
- Masking tape: 6 to 8 rolls (Sessions 1–5)
- Turtle Turners: 1 per pair (Sessions 2–3). See Other Preparation for directions on making Turtle Turners.
- 12"-by-2" strips cut from red construction paper: 15 per student plus 20–30 for the teacher (Sessions 4–5)
- Computers with *Geo-Logo* installed (Sessions 2–8)
- Overhead projector (Sessions 2–8)

Other Preparation

- Duplicate student sheets and teaching resources (located at the end of this unit) in the following quantities. If you have Student Activity Booklets, copy only the items marked with an asterisk.

For Session 1

Student Sheet 11, A Neighborhood Path (p. 145): 1 per student (homework)

For Sessions 2–3

Turtle Turners* (p. 159): 1 transparency for every 4 students. Cut each transparency into 4 Turtle Turners.

Turtle Turner Pointers* (p. 160): Copy onto oaktag or construction paper. Cut each apart. Attach the pointers to Turtle Turners with paper fasteners.

Geo-Logo User Sheet* (p. 161): Post one copy beside each computer.

Student Sheet 12, Maze Commands (p. 146): 1 per student, plus 1 transparency*

Student Sheet 13, Turtle Turns 1 (p. 147): 1 per student, plus 1 transparency*

Student Sheet 14, Turtle Turns 2 (p. 148): 1 per student, plus 1 transparency*

Student Sheet 15, Walking a Path at Home (p. 149): 1 per student (homework)

For Sessions 4–5

Student Sheet 16, Today's Number (p. 150): 1 per student (homework)

For Sessions 6–8

Student Sheet 17, Andy the Ant Problems (p. 151): 1 per student

Student Sheet 18, Andy the Ant's Paths (p. 152): 1 per student, plus 1 transparency*

Student Sheet 19, Allison the Ant Problems (p. 153): 1 per student

Student Sheet 20, Allison the Ant's Paths (p. 154): 1 per student, plus 1 transparency*

Continued on next page

Student Sheet 21, More Allison the Ant Problems (p. 155): 1 per student

Student Sheet 22, More Allison the Ant's Paths (p. 156): 1 per student

Student Sheet 23, Tina the Turtle Game Commands (p. 157): 1–2 per student

Student Sheet 24, Three Paths for Andy the Ant (p. 158): 1 per student (homework)

■ Prepare three masking-tape paths on the classroom floor. (Or you may want to use the hallway, cafeteria, or gym.) Choose three sets of landmarks—for example, the door and bookshelf, the meeting area and bulletin board, and the door and window. Include both left and right turns and straight lines in the paths. (Session 1)

■ If not done previously, install *Geo-Logo* on each available computer. (See p. 129 in the *Geo-Logo* Teacher Tutorial.) See the **Teacher Note,** Managing the Computer Activities (p. 22), for suggestions about how to incorporate the computer activities into the curriculum, depending on the number of computers available to you. (Sessions 2–8)

■ Work through the *Geo-Logo* Teacher Tutorial (p. 93) and try the activities your-self before introducing them to students. (Sessions 2–8)

■ Cut 12" strips of red construction paper by cutting 9"-by-12" construction paper along its 12" dimension. Strips should be about 2" wide. Students will use these to make paths in the classroom. Prepare about 15 strips for each student and about 30 extras. If you work outside the classroom or have students make longer paths, you may need more paper strips. (Sessions 4–5)

■ Use your red paper strips to make two paths on the classroom floor, such as the ones shown in Session 4 (p. 63). Each path should start at the same place. One path should be straight. The other path should cover a shorter distance than the straight path but have several turns in it, thus using more units than the straight path. Place strips end to end and tape into position. (Sessions 4–5)

Walking, Visualizing, and Representing Paths

What Happens

Students walk paths in their classroom and describe their movements. After walking a path in the gym or on the playground, they record their paths and then follow their representations and describe their movements. Their work focuses on:

■ moving along a path

■ visualizing and then representing a path

Start-Up

Today's Number

■ **Calendar Date** If you are using the calendar date for Today's Number, brainstorm with students ways to express the number. Suggest students use combinations of 10 in their number sentences. For example, if today's number is 23 and one number sentence is 10 + 10 + 3, ask students if there is another way of making 10, such as (6 + 4) + (6 + 4) + 3, or (4 + 3 + 2 + 1) + (4 + 3 + 2 + 1) + 3. Record their expressions on chart paper.

■ **Number of School Days** If you are using the number of school days for Today's Number, and the number is over 100, focus on ways to make 100 using multiples of 5 and 10. For example, if the number is 138, a solution is 25 + 25 + 20 + 20 + 10 + 35 + 3. Add a card to the class counting strip and fill in another number on the 200 chart.

How Many Pockets? The routine How Many Pockets? gives students an opportunity to collect, represent, and interpret numerical data through an experience that is meaningful to them. As students collect data about pockets throughout the year, they create natural opportunities to compare quantities and to see that data can change over time.

This routine is one that occurs regularly throughout the *Investigations* curriculum. The complete write-up of this routine, which includes several versions, can be found on p. 85. If you are doing the full-year grade 2 *Investigations* curriculum, students will be familiar with this routine, and you should proceed with the following activity. If this is your first *Investigations* unit, familiarize yourself with this routine, and do the basic pocket activity with students *instead* of the following activity.

Materials

■ Masking tape (6–8 rolls)

■ Adding machine tape (6–8 rolls)

■ Crayons, markers

■ Sidewalk chalk (optional)

■ Clipboards (optional)

■ Carpet remnants, traffic cones or large geometric shapes cut from poster board (optional)

■ Student Sheet 11 (1 per student, homework)

■ Drawing paper (at least 1 per student)

■ **Calculating the Total Number of Pockets** Divide students into groups of four or five. Ask each group to find the total number of pockets they are wearing. Then collect the data from each group and record it on the board. Using this information, students work in pairs to determine the total number of pockets being worn by the class. Ask students to share the strategies they used to find the total.

Introducing Paths

Begin this investigation by introducing the idea of paths and pathways to your students. See the **Teacher Note**, Paths and Shapes (p. 51).

In the next few math classes we are going to be constructing, measuring, and drawing simple paths around our classroom and around the school. How would you describe what a path is?

Once the idea of a path is established, have students visualize a path in the school as you describe it in words. Choose a path that is familiar to students with a destination that is not too far away from your classroom. Consider such routes as from the classroom to the library or the cafeteria.

I want you to close your eyes and imagine that you are walking from our classroom to the library. As I tell you the story of our trip, see if you imagine the path that we are taking.

Describe the trip for students noting special landmarks such as classrooms, water fountains, bulletin boards, stairways, and any turns you make.

Note: *The Red Carpet* by Rex Parkin (1993, Aladdin [a division of Macmillan Children's Book Group]) is a nice way to introduce the idea of paths to your students. Although the book is now out of print, check your school or public library to try to locate a copy.

Walking Paths in the Classroom

Show students the masking-tape paths you have made on the classroom floor (or the hallway, cafeteria, or gym).

These are some of the paths I walked earlier today. This path is how I walked from our classroom door to the bookshelf. This one goes from the meeting area to the bulletin board. And this one goes from the door to the window.

As students watch, walk along one of the paths. As you walk, ask a volunteer to describe your movements and direction—when you walk forward or straight ahead, and when you turn left or right.

Next, have one or two students walk along each path as another student describes their movements. Leave the paths on the floor so that all students can walk them at some point during Sessions 1 and 2 or at other times during the school day.

Walking and Drawing Paths

You may want to do this activity on the playground or, in case of inclement weather, in the gym or cafeteria. If your class size is small, the activity can be done in the classroom.

Note: If you do this activity in the gym, you may want to set up locations on the gym floor. For instance, you could place carpet remnants or traffic cones or shapes cut from poster board in different locations around the room.

With the students gathered around you on the playground (or in the gym or classroom), generate several paths students could walk. Choose one path to focus on; this example uses a path from the school doors to the jungle gym.

Imagine that you are walking from the school doors to the jungle gym. You walk past the swings on your way. [*Point out each of the places on the playground.*] **What will your path be like? Think carefully and try to picture in your mind how you would walk that path.**

Invite students to describe the path they would walk. Encourage them to think about when they make turns and when they walk straight and to describe any landmarks along the way. Students may not be accurate—visualizing a path can be a difficult task. (Many adults find giving street directions difficult.) The purpose here is to help students become aware of paths and to begin to visualize their movement along a path.

❖ **Tips for a Linguistically Diverse Classroom**   To ensure that students with a limited English proficiency understand the specific task, draw pictures of the key places they are passing in the scenario on the chalkboard (school doors, swings, jungle gym). Instead of verbally describing the path they visualize, ask students to draw a picture of what the path might be like.

In just a minute, we'll walk from the school doors, past the swings, to the jungle gym. As we walk, think carefully about our path. Try to remember when we walk straight and when we make turns. When we finish walking, I'll ask you to describe the path we walked.

Note: You may want to have small groups of students walk the path at one time, rather than the whole class.

Give students the opportunity to describe the path they walked. Then explain that, working in pairs, they will walk a path on the playground and record their paths. (If students are walking paths on blacktop or cement, they can use sidewalk chalk to record their paths. If they are working in the gym, they can use adding machine tape or masking tape.)

Partners should then walk the path they recorded. As one student walks, the other should describe his or her movements in terms of direction, for example, walking straight and turning right.

Next have pairs of students team up, and in a similar manner walk and describe each other's path. Each pair of students should discuss their paths, noting likenesses and differences. This is an opportunity for students to verbalize their spatial thinking. Not only does this help them use and acquire language and make sense of spatial concepts, but it also exposes them to other ways of describing and representing spatial relationships.

After students have described their paths, you may want to have them draw their paths on paper. Expect a wide range of drawings. Students may draw a picture of a path rather than a maplike drawing. See the **Dialogue Box**, Walking and Drawing Paths (p. 52), for examples of how students have talked about their paths.

Session 1 Follow-Up

 **Homework**

A Neighborhood Path   Students visualize and describe in words on Student Sheet 11 a familiar path they take in their neighborhood. They should include turns and any landmarks, such as a doorstep, fire hydrant, playground, or apple tree.

 **Extension**

Walking a Path in Our School   Students visualize and then walk to a familiar place in the school—for example, from the classroom to the library. They return to the classroom and draw their paths. After comparing and discussing their recordings, they walk again to the library, this time comparing their drawings to the actual walk. When they return to the classroom, they make any revisions that are needed.

Paths and Shapes

We use the idea of *paths* all the time. We walk on paths, drive certain paths to familiar places, and even follow a path, or line, of reasoning. What is a path in mathematics? It is a representation or record of movement. A path is made by moving the pencil on paper, without lifting it and without retracing any of the movement.

A *straight path* is a path that results from movement without turns.

Lines and line segments can be thought of as straight paths; that is, lines are all the places you could move, going forward or backward as far as you want without any turning; segments are like lines with boundaries or roadblock.

A *turn* is a rotation or change in direction. A turn creates a corner in a path.

A *closed path* is a path whose starting and ending points are the same.

In this investigation, students make and measure simple paths. In the first activities, students estimate distances of straight paths, first with one unit of length, then with several units.

When students use *Geo-Logo*, the units of length are "turtle steps," which can change in size for different activities. Students estimate these units as they move the turtle, then direct the turtle through mazes to learn more about turns, lengths, and paths. Students' work with paths and *Geo-Logo* is continued and developed in the grade 3 unit, *Turtle Paths*.

Finally, students use what they know to make pictures and designs. Every path has a shape. Shape is the form or contour of anything. Some paths have forms we recognize as "common shapes" such as rectangles, squares, or triangles.

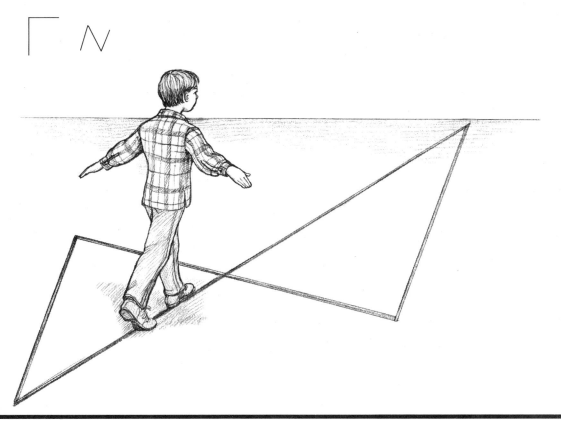

Walking and Drawing Paths

The students in this second grade walked and recorded paths on the playground. This class demonstrated a range of awareness about representing movement through space. Some students omitted parts of the paths in their drawings. For some, turns seemed to represent stopping points that did not include information about direction. Some students marked off steps when no landmarks were available. Also, many students' drawings have inconsistent perspectives. Their paths look like they are drawn from a bird's-eye view, but their landmarks are drawn from a side view, almost like a picture rather than a map.

Paul saw his walk as movement from one piece of playground equipment to another. He did not include turns in his drawing. All landmarks are drawn from a side view.

Jess and Bjorn made a more sophisticated drawing, then corrected it when they saw the first drawing didn't match their actual path. They walked from the doors to the tetherball pole, right to the jungle gym, right to the end of the cement, then left to the swings. Jess draws a path to represent their walk. First he draws the landmarks in the order the boys encountered them. Then he draws a path through the landmarks.

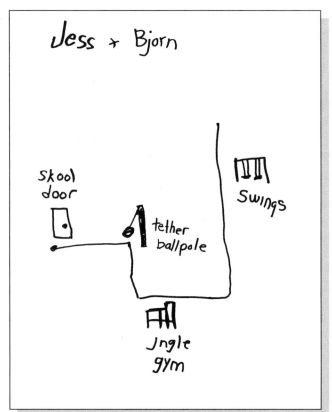

The boys walk the path again with their drawing in hand, this time comparing their drawing to the actual walk. Jess and Bjorn correct the position of some landmarks as they walk.

Continued on next page

continued

Bjorn: The tetherball pole should be here. Here, we're wrong [*Bjorn points to the drawing of the path*]; we only go past the tetherball pole. In the walk, we go around it, and turn *this* way [*he gestures left, toward the jungle gym*]. Then we walk to the jungle gym.

The boys try the drawing again, changing the first turn from right to left. They move the position of the jungle gym. They correct their drawing by reflecting on the landmark in relation to the path they walked. The boys continue their walk, checking their drawing as they go. After making the turn at the cement, Jess realizes that the swing set is in the wrong location on the drawing.

Jess: We're not going to go by the swing set [*as he has shown in his drawing*].

Jess repositions the swing set in his drawing.

Overall, Jess and Bjorn did well with their drawing. Originally, they included the correct number of straight parts in their path, although they drew their first turn in the wrong direction and misplaced a few of the landmarks. However, they were able to correct their drawing as they walked the path a second time.

Jess enjoyed drawing the playground path so much that he went home and walked another path in the park. He brought his drawing of his path to share with the class the next day.

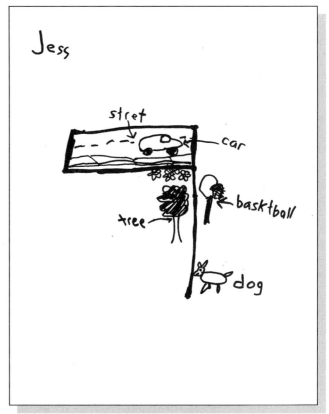

Investigating Turns

Materials

- *Geo-Logo* User Sheet (1 posted at each computer)
- Student Sheet 12 (1 per student)
- Student Sheets 13 and 14 (1 of each per student)
- Transparency of Student Sheets 12–14 (1 of each)
- Prepared Turtle Turners (1 per student)
- Masking tape
- Computers with *Geo-Logo* installed
- Overhead projector (optional)
- Student Sheet 15 (1 per student, homework)

What Happens

Students turn their bodies and describe how many units they have turned. They use a Turtle Turner to help them estimate and measure turtle turns and are introduced to Maze, a computer activity in which students move the *Geo-Logo* turtle along a path. Their work focuses on:

- understanding turns as a change in orientation or heading
- exploring what happens when turns are repeated
- describing turns in terms of units

Start-Up

Today's Number

Calendar Date *and* Number of School Days   Students can express Today's Number using doubles. For example, if the number is 28 (calendar date), possible expressions are 14 + 14, 7 + 7 + 7 + 7, 10 + 10 + 4 + 4, and so on. If Today's Number is over 100, such as 139, possible expressions are: 50 + 50 + 15 + 15 + 4 + 4 + 1 or 70 + 70 − 1. If you are counting the number of school days, add a card to the counting strip and fill in the next number on the blank 200 chart.

Activity

Turning Your Body

Note: This activity introduces students to left and right turning movements, which they will use in the computer activity Maze.

Ask students to explain what a turn is. Some may suggest that it is a change in direction or heading. For additional information about turns, see the **Teacher Note**, Turns (p. 62).

For this activity, students should be standing and facing the front of the room. Ask them to hold out their right hands, then turn right all the way around until they are facing the front again. Repeat for left turns. Next, direct students' attention to a clock. You may want to record some of the commands you just tried on the chalkboard.

When a hand on the clock moves from 12 to 1 (from straight up to the right), that is r1. "R" means right. From 12 to 2 on a clock is r2. What command would turn a hand from 12 to 6 (from straight up to straight down)? (r6) What command would turn a hand from 12 all the way around to 12 again? (r12)

After a few other examples, ask students to face the front of the room, then turn like a clock, r12. Repeat with r6, then another r6. Ask students to tell where they are facing. (front) Try r3. Where are they facing? (right wall) Repeat r3 commands three more times, until students are facing the front wall. Continue giving a few other commands.

■ **Turn r3 and r3 again. What is one command that will face us to the front of the room again? (r6)**

■ **How many r3 turns do I have to make to turn all the way around? (4) What one command could I give for that? (r12)**

■ **Turn r2. What command will take you to r4? (another r2)**

■ **Turn l3 [*read "el three"*]. Do another l3. Where are you facing? (the back of the room; l6) What other way(s) could you have turned to face that way? (r3 and r3; r6)**

You may want to lay out a large clockface without numerals on the class-room floor. Represent each turn unit with a piece of masking tape. Mark one piece of tape (or use colored tape or tape a small piece of colored paper into place) to identify the starting position. Students can take turns standing in the center of the clockface and using the markings to help them turn.

Or use a game spinner as a model. Give each pair of students a Turtle Turner. Tell students that this is a special kind of spinner and to use it as they gently turn the pointer. Have each pair place their Turtle Turner in front of them, with the arrow pointing to up. As you give turn commands, have students turn the pointer on the Turtle Turner, then move their bodies in a similar way. For more information about turns in grade 2, see the **Teacher Note,** Turns (p. 62).

On-Computer Activity: Introducing Maze

Note: If you are using Investigation 2 separately from Investigation 1, see the **Teacher Note**, Spatial Sense and Geometry with *Geo-Logo* (p. 23), for information about how this software contributes to students' learning in mathematics. Also, you should work through the *Geo-Logo* Teacher Tutorial and do the Maze activity (p. 103) before working on the computer with students. Post copies of the *Geo-Logo* User Sheet next to each computer.

Gather students around the demonstration computer. Remind them how to open the *Geo-Logo* software and choose the Maze activity.

Today we're going to instruct the turtle to travel through a maze. Our turtle has to find the baby turtle who has wandered off and lost herself in the maze, then bring her home. Our turtle has only a certain amount of energy and if he uses it up before finding the baby, he has to start at the beginning all over again.

Point out the turtle at the start of the maze and the gauge just above the maze. Explain that as the turtle moves through the maze, he uses energy. The gauge shows how much energy is left.

Look at the maze and the paths in it, and talk about how the turtle will have to move through the maze to reach the baby.

Besides moving forward, such as in the Steps activity, what will the turtle have to do? (move backward, turn) **The command b is the opposite of forward. What do you think b stands for?** (back or backward)

Introduce the turn command r (right turn) and ʟ (left turn). Students must enter a number to tell the turtle how far to turn. The numbers they enter will turn the turtle, just as they turned their bodies in the previous activity and just like the hands of a clock or the Turtle Turner turn.

We can rescue the baby turtle, now that we know all the commands: two that move the turtle forward and backward, f and b, and two that turn the turtle right and left, r and ʟ. Remember, you have only so much energy to save the baby, so make good estimates of the distance to go forward or backward and how far to turn.

Ask students what commands to enter to begin moving the turtle. As you type them in, name each key you press.

We want to go forward 3 turtle steps, so I'll type f **<space>** 3 then press
<return>.

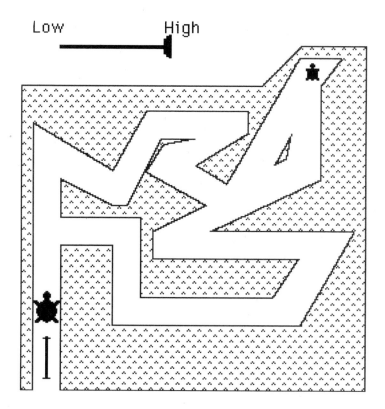

Enter commands that students suggest, without evaluating them in any
way.

Note: The main purpose of this demonstration is to show students how to
use commands and tools in *Geo-Logo*. You don't need to reach the baby in
this demonstration.

Commands can be edited, such as changing f 3 to f 6.

**If I haven't pressed <return>, I can change anything I already typed. I
use the mouse or the arrow keys to move the cursor in the Command
Center to be beside the 3, press <delete> to remove the 3, and type 6.
When I press <return> I see what this command will do—the turtle runs
the new commands and so now the first line segment is 6 turtle steps
long.**

Commands such as f 4 and f 2 can be combined into a single command. Ask
students what command you could use to move the turtle forward the total

distance of 4 and 2. Demonstrate how clicking on the **Erase One tool** 🔲 in
the Tool bar erases the last command f 2; then use **<delete>** to remove the
4, and type 6.

Show how to use the **Line of Sight tool** . Point out that the arrow indicates the turtle's direction, and you can count the number of turn units you wish to turn using the rays (help students count the rotation from one ray to another, rather than the rays themselves). It may help to have students recall how they turned in the body-turning activity.

To make our turtle turn right I will type r **for right turn.**

Ask students to suggest how far the turtle should turn to continue moving along the path, then try their suggestions. Continue along the path.

Demonstrate how clicking on the **Erase All tool** starts the activity over again. Point out how the turtle's unit length may change. Explain that students can challenge themselves by solving the maze with different unit lengths. They can change the unit length to another number by changing the number after the stepsize command. The stepsizes that will be accepted are 1, 2, and 3. Suggest they start with the stepsize 1.

Tell students that as they work at the computer, they are to record their commands on Student Sheet 12, Maze Commands. Show how to do this by writing in the commands that have been entered on the computer on a transparency or on the board. Then remind students how to save their work at the end of a computer session.

You will want to save your work so that you can begin where you left off the next time you use the computer. Remember to include these things in the work you save: initials for you and your partner, the activity name, and the date.

For a review of how to save an activity, see On-Computer Activity: Introducing Steps (p. 14). A further explanation is given in the Teacher Tutorial (p. 113).

Explain that during this session and the next one, students will have the opportunity to use this activity on the computer.

Turning Turtles

In this off-computer activity, students become familiar with the turns the turtle can make in *Geo-Logo*. Provide each pair of students with a Turtle Turner.

Demonstrate the activity by putting a Turtle Turner on the overhead projector and ask students to describe it. Ask volunteers to use the Turtle Turners on the overhead to illustrate turns of r 1 through r 6 and then ι 1 through ι 6.

Using a transparency of Student Sheet 13, demonstrate how to place the Turtle Turner in the same direction as a turtle on the student sheet with the center of the Turtle Turner directly on the center of the turtle. Point out the target the turtle must turn toward. Together find how many turn units the turtle must turn to reach the object.

Explain that on Student Sheets 13 and 14, partners first predict how many turn units each turtle must turn to reach the target object. Each student records his or her prediction on the student sheet. To find out how far each turtle must turn to reach the target object, students put the Turtle Turner directly over the turtle, facing in the same direction, then turn the Turtle Turner until it points directly to the object. Students will record the turn the turtle must make (for example, r 3) to reach the target on the student sheet.

You may want to provide students with Student Sheets 13 and 14 at this time. These sheets can be placed in their math folders and saved for when they work on this activity during Choice Time.

Choice Time

Post the following choices on the chalkboard:

> 1. Turning Turtles
>
> 2. Maze (computer)

Students will be working on Choice Time activities for the remainder of today's session and during the next math class.

Choice 1: Turning Turtles

Materials: Student Sheets 13 and 14, Turtle Turns 1 and 2; Turtle Turners

In this off-computer activity, students first predict how far the turtles shown on Turtle Turns 1 and 2 must go to reach a target. Then they use their Turtle Turners to determine how far the turtle's actual turn must be. They line up the Turtle Turner on top of each turtle shown on their student sheets and turn the pointer until it is pointing directly to the object. Students should record the turn the turtle must make.

Choice 2: Maze

Materials: Computer with *Geo-Logo* installed; Student Sheet 12, Maze Commands

Pairs of students play the game Maze. One student enters commands into the computer, as a partner records the commands on Student Sheet 12. Partners can switch roles about every 5 minutes. Encourage students to refer to the *Geo-Logo* User Sheet posted beside each computer.

Observing the Students

As you watch students work, use the following questions to help you evaluate their understanding.

Turning Turtles

- How do students predict how far the turtle must turn?
- Do some students think about "landmark" turns such as r 3 and r 6 to make their predictions? (Do they recognize when a target is a little more than 3 turn units away from the starting point?)
- Are students able to make predictions and measure turns when the turtle's starting point changes? If so, how?

- Do they align the turtle turner so that it faces in the same direction? Or do they count on from the turtle's position? (For example, if the turtle is facing r 3 and turns to r 5, do they count r 4, r 5 to determine that the turtle turns right 2 units?)

Maze

You will probably need to spend most of your time helping students get started and enter commands on the computer.

- Do students move and turn the turtle only by trial and error?
- Do students consistently move in increments of only 1 or 2? (These students may need more opportunity simply to play the game, without the added challenge of the Maze problems. As they play, encourage them to examine and combine their commands when possible.)
- Can students estimate distances and turns? Are students able to reach the baby turtle without running out of energy? Do they combine commands readily?
- Are students using strategies to estimate length?
- How are students estimating turns? Are they using the hours of the clock to help them visualize how to turn the turtle? (For example, "If the turtle turns from 12:00 to 6:00, the command is r 6." "If the turtle turns from 6:00 to 4:00, the command is l 2."
- Are students combining commands to save energy? For example, do they combine commands such as r 2 r 2 into one r 4; or f 2 f 1 into a single f 3?

The following are some additional notes on tools.

- **Teach Tool** If a pair of students completes the Maze, show the pair how to use the **Teach tool** to teach the turtle their solution. After clicking on this tool, a dialog box asks for solution name. Name the solution and then demonstrate how to run it by entering its name in the Command Center. (**Note:** Students must use **<delete>** to delete the "stepsize" command *before* they enter their procedure name and press **<return>**.)
- **Saving Work** As students finish this activity, you may want them to save their work either on a disk or on the computer's internal drive. Gather several pairs around one computer to demonstrate this, then ask them to go back and try saving their work.

This is a good time for students to record in their Weekly Logs. Encourage them to share any questions they are having about the work. Remind them to record which activities they chose during this Choice Time and to record the work they did.

Note: Remember to set up the red paper paths in the classroom for the next session. See Other Preparation, p. 46, for more information.

Sessions 2 and 3 Follow-Up

Homework

Walking a Path at Home Students write a description of a familiar path they walk at home on Student Sheet 15, Walking a Path at Home. They should also draw the path. For instance, a student might describe a path such as this one: To get from my bedroom to the living room, I walk straight down the hall, I turn left after the bathroom, and walk down the stairs. Then I turn left again and walk straight into the living room.

❖ **Tip for the Linguistically Diverse Classroom** Suggest that students use the following code and draw their path instead of writing one:

S for *straight*   LT for *left turn*   RT for *right turn*

Suggest also that students draw pictures of what they might pass in a path they walk at home. They can create rebuses of a bedroom, hall, bathroom, stairs, living room, and kitchen.

Teacher Note   *Turns*

The idea of turns is difficult for students. The *Investigations* curriculum develops the ideas of turn and angle and measurement of turns and angles in the second through fifth grades. In second grade, the goals for students are to:

- distinguish between turns (that make bends) in paths and forward and backward movements (that make line segments)
- distinguish between right and left turns
- compare turns, identifying "more turning" and "less turning"
- gain initial experience estimating the measure of turns using simple units

The turn units used in second grade are related to turns in degrees. Thus, when we give the turtle commands such as r1, r2, and r3, the turtle makes the corresponding turns—a right 30° turn,

a right 60° turn, and a right 90° turn, respectively. In grades 3 through 5, describing turns becomes more sophisticated as students work with angles and degrees.

In this grade, trial and error is still an acceptable approach to turn problems; students will have additional opportunities with turns and turn measurement in later grades.

Measuring Paths

What Happens

Students use paper strips to construct and then compare two paths between the same places—one path is straight and the other path has turns. They describe where their paths go and how long each path is. This activity is used as a Teacher Checkpoint. Their work focuses on:

■ determining path length by iterating and counting units

■ comparing lengths of paths by comparing the number of units used to measure each path

■ understanding turns as a change in orientation or heading

■ exploring what happens when turns are repeated

■ describing turns in terms of units

Start-Up

Today's Number

Calendar Date *and* Number of School Days   Students can express Today's Number using coins (pennies, nickels, dimes, quarters). For example, if the number is 31 (calendar date), possible combinations are: 25¢ + 5¢ + 1¢ or 10¢ + 10¢ + 10¢ + 1¢. If Today's Number is over 100, such as 140, a possible combination is 25¢ + 25¢ + 25¢ + 25¢ + 25¢ + 10¢ + 5¢. If you are counting the number of school days, add a card to the class counting strip and fill in another number on the blank 200 chart.

Homework   Students share the descriptions of the paths they wrote for homework in groups. Student work can be displayed in the classroom.

Materials

■ Masking tape

■ 12" red paper strips (about 15 per student, plus 25–30 extra)

■ Student Sheet 12 (1 per student)

■ Computers with *Geo-Logo* installed

■ Overhead projector

■ Transparency of Student Sheet 12

■ Student Sheet 16 (1 per student, homework)

Activity

Comparing Lengths of Paths

Show students a few of the red paper strips and demonstrate that they are of equal length. Point out the two paper paths that you made on the classroom floor. As in the examples shown here, one path should cover a shorter

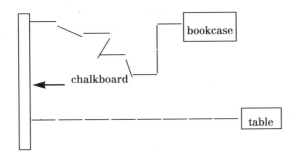

distance than the other but have several turns in it, making it longer than the straight path. If possible, both paths should start at the same place.

Two paths are on the floor today. I'm going to ask two students to walk on the paths. Watch carefully and see if you can tell who walks farther. Don't say anything yet. We'll talk about it in a few minutes.

After one student walks on the first path, have another student walk on the second path.

Rosie walked from the chalkboard to the bookcase, and Chen walked from the chalkboard to the table. Who do you think walked farther, Rosie or Chen? How can you tell?

Encourage students to explain their thinking. Using this example, some may say Chen walked farther because the distance between the chalkboard and the table is longer than the distance from the chalkboard to the bookcase. Other students may see that one path has more paper strips than the other, so that the student who walked this path actually walked farther. Ask students how many paper strips are in each path, and discuss what makes one path longer than the other.

The path that has many turns requires more strips, actually making it longer. Some students may have difficulty understanding this because when they consider length, they focus on the endpoints. To help students consider how the paths are arranged, you might have them walk each path and count and compare the number of strips in the paths. You might also rearrange the strips in the path with turns so that both paths are straight, then ask students to count the strips in each path and determine which is longer. See the **Dialogue Box,** Comparing Lengths of Paths (p. 69), for examples of students' thinking about length and units.

During the rest of this session and in the next session, students will have more experiences comparing paths.

Activity

Introducing Paper Paths

Introduce this activity now, so students can work independently during Choice Time. Since the activity requires considerable space, you might use the hallway in addition to your classroom space or a larger location in the school building.

Provide pairs of students with several of the paper strips.

During Choice Time, you will use paper strips like these to build paths. Some of you will work in the classroom, and others will work in the hallway. Let's list some places where we can build paths. We need to say where the path will start and where it will end.

Brainstorm a list of starting points and ending points, recording them on chart paper. Since one path students build will be straight, the starting and ending points should have no obstacle between them. When the list is complete, have students choose (or you can assign) the path they will build. List their names next to the path they choose. For some starting and ending points, have two pairs of students building paths. This will allow for comparisons of paths to be made. (This is not necessary for all paths.) Some students might also prefer to invent paths that are not listed on the chart.

Paths

door to windows: Ayaz & Laura & Harris

chalkboard to windows: Carla & Lila, Temara & Graham

reading corner to chalkboard: Jess & Tim, Tory & Chen

door to Mr. Ho's room: Franco & Rosie & Karina

closet to bulletin board: Angel & Simon

door to Ms. Clark's room: Helena & Phoebe, Salim & Ping

door to water fountain: Juanita & Jeffrey & Trini

bookcase to bulletin board: Olga & Paul & Linda

meeting area to windows: Naomi & Imani & Lionel

You will work with your partner or group to build two paths—a straight path and a path with turns. After you finish your paths, you will figure out how many paper strips long each one is. Then each of you will draw and write about your paths. You will tell how long each one is, then describe the paths and tell how they are different.

Collect the paper strips. Provide pairs or groups with enough strips during Choice Time.

On-Computer Activity: More About Maze

When most students have had an opportunity to do the Maze game on the computer one or two times and record their commands of one game on Student Sheet 12, explain how they will continue work on the activity during Choice Time. Gather students around the demonstration computer and the overhead projector. Open *Geo-Logo* and choose the Maze activity.

Place a transparency of Maze Commands on the overhead. Choose one pair to bring their copy of Maze Commands up and draw one way they completed the maze. Record the first few commands they used on the transparency.

In all the games we have done so far, the turtle takes the same-size steps. We can make the turtle take bigger steps by changing the stepsize in the Command Center to 2 or 3.

Ebony and Olga started their maze by using these commands. If we want the turtle to walk the same path as before, but we change the stepsize to 2, what should our first commands be?

Record suggested commands on the transparency under Game 2 and demonstrate on the computer. Students may want to correct the commands if the turtle doesn't move as they wish.

Tell students that if they've recorded one of their paths and its commands on Student Sheet 12, they are to change the stepsize to 2 or 3 and write commands that will take the turtle along the same pathway.

Also discuss some of the ways they can find the length of the paths. Point out and click on the **Label Lengths tool** . Talk about the label that appears on the turtle's step, and tell students that this is the unit length. Enter a forward command, for example   f **<space>** 3 **<return>**, to move the turtle forward. The distance the turtle moved forward is labeled "3." Ask students how they could use this information to find the length of the turtle's path. They may see that they can add the lengths the turtle moves to find the total path length.

Note: The **Label Lengths tool** can be applied before any commands are entered or at any time during the game.

To find each path's length in different units (stepsizes 1, 2, and 3), remind students that they can change the turtle's stepsize by changing the number after the stepsize command. The stepsize command is the first command in the Command Center, and it appears each time the game is played.

Remind students that as they play, partners also record the commands on the student sheet.

Choice Time

Students will work on Choice Time activities during the rest of today's and tomorrow's sessions. Post the following list of activities:

---

1. Turning Turtles

2. Maze (computer)

3. More About Maze (computer)

4. Making and Comparing
   Paper Paths

When new choices are added to the list, students may be eager to try the new activity first. The quantity of materials may limit the number of students that can do an activity at one time. Even if this is not the case, limit the number of students who work at an activity at one time. This encourages students to make decisions about what they are going to do. It also provides an opportunity to return to some choices. Choice 4 is a Teacher Checkpoint, so try to observe all students working on this choice. Be sure all students complete that activity.

For a review of Choice 1: Turning Turtles, and Choice 2: Maze, and suggestions about what to observe as students work, see p. 60.

Choice 3: More About Maze

Materials: Computers with *Geo-Logo* installed; Student Sheet 12, Maze Commands

Students change the stepsize to 2 or 3 and write new commands to follow the same path. Taking turns, one student enters commands on the computer while the other records them on the student sheet under Game 2. When finished, the pair finds the total length of both parts.

Choice 4: Making and Comparing Paper Paths

Materials: 12" red paper strips, masking tape, paper

Working in pairs or small groups, students build two different paths between two endpoints—a straight path and a path with turns in it. They place paper strips end to end on the floor, and when they are satisfied with the paths they have constructed, they tape the strips into position. Students compare their paths, finding the length of each in paper strip units, and then draw and write about the paths.

Note: Since this activity is used as a Teacher Checkpoint, all students should complete it during Choice Time.

Observing the Students

As you watch students work, think about the following:

More About Maze

If students are still going through the maze and recording their commands for the first time, suggestions for observing them are on p. 61. If students are doing the More About Maze activity, observe the following:

- How do students find the number of steps to include in a forward command? Do they use trial and error? Do they estimate the number of steps using the picture of the new stepsize? Do they use commands from their first game to help them plan the number of steps for their second game?

- Do students realize that the turn amounts stay the same even though the stepsize changes?

- How do students find the total lengths of their paths? Do they use the **Label Lengths tool**? How do they combine the lengths for the different path segments? Do they see any relationship between the lengths of the paths for Games 1 and 2?

Making and Comparing Paper Paths

This activity can be used as a Teacher Checkpoint. Observe how students use strips to make paths by iterating units.

- As students build their paths, how do they place the strips? Are the strips placed end to end? Are there gaps between strips, or are strips overlapping?

- How do students plan and build their paths? Do some students build more complex paths, such as paths with several turns?

- How do students represent their paths when drawn? Do the number of strips and the directions of turns match their actual paths?

Sessions 4 and 5 Follow-Up

 **Homework**

Today's Number Students record Today's Number in the blank on Student Sheet 16. For homework, they find five ways to make Today's Number using combinations of 10. For example, 33 = 6 + 4 + 6 + 4 + 6 + 4 + 3, or 33 = 1 + 9 + 3 + 7 + 2 + 8 + 3.

Comparing Lengths of Paths

In this discussion, students are comparing two paths that the teacher has constructed on the floor, similar to the paths shown on p. 63. Students have compared the paper strips used to make the paths and concluded that the units are equal in size. As students compare the paths, confusion arises and language ambiguities emerge when the number of units in each path and the lengths of the paths are considered.

Rosie walked from the chalkboard to the book-case, and Chen walked from the chalkboard to the table. Who do you think took more steps, Rosie or Chen? How can you tell?

Tim: I think Chen walked farther.

Why do you think so, Tim?

Tim: Because the table is farther away from the chalkboard than the bookcase is.

What do other people think?

Laura: I think Rosie walked farther. I counted the paper strips when they were walking on them, and Rosie's [path] has more.

Carla: But Rosie only walked to the bookcase, and Chen walked to the table. It's farther to the table.

Is everyone convinced that Rosie's path has more paper strips?

A few students say yes, but several are unsure.

Let's have two people walk the paths, one at a time. Lila? Simon? This time, when Lila and Simon walk, we'll count the paper strips they walk on.

The class counts 10 paper strips as Simon walks the path to the bookcase, and 8 paper strips when Lila walks to the table.

This is an interesting problem. How can Simon's path have more paper strips? The table Lila walked to is farther away. What do people think?

Trini: Well, Lila's path is straight, and Simon made lots of turns. Maybe turns make you use up more paper strips.

Trini's idea is that the path with turns might use more paper strips. Let's think about that. Remember what happened when we measured the width of our classroom? Some students used more cubes than others did. Do you remember why?

Karina: Because some people didn't go straight across the room. They went around desks and stuff.

Chen: Some people made turns, and that made them use more cubes.

So when we measured the classroom, making turns used more cubes. How is that like this problem?

Karina: I guess when you make turns, instead of going straight, you have to take more steps.

Harris: The turns made Simon take more steps, so he walked farther.

Tim: But I still think Chen walked *farther* because the table is farther away from the board than the bookcase.

[*A few students nod in agreement.*]

Language and vocabulary can often become a factor in students' understanding of a problem. In this dialogue, many students were able to distinguish between "farther away" and "number of paper strips," but some focused on the endpoints of the path and could not see how the arrangement of the path was related to its length, the actual distance walked.

Moving on a Grid

Materials

- Student Sheets 17 and 18 (1 of each per student)
- Student Sheets 19 and 20 (1 of each per student)
- Student Sheet 21 (1 per student)
- Student Sheet 22 (1 per student)
- Student Sheet 23 (1–2 per student)
- Overhead projector
- Transparencies of Student Sheets 18 and 20
- Computers with *Geo-Logo* installed
- Student Sheet 24 (1 per student, homework)

What Happens

Students compare lengths of paths represented on grid paper. They then plan and draw their own paths on grid paper and determine the length of the paths. A computer activity also provides students with experience with paths on grids. Their work focuses on:

- interpreting and comparing representations of paths on a grid
- constructing paths on a grid

Start-Up

Today's Number

- **Calendar Date** If you are using the calendar date for Today's Number, brainstorm with students ways to express the number. Suggest students use combinations of 10 in their number sentences. For example, if today's number is 23 and one number sentence is $10 + 10 + 3$, ask students if there is another way of making 10, such as $(6 + 4) + (6 + 4) + 3$, or $(4 + 3 + 2 + 1) + (4 + 3 + 2 + 1) + 3$. Record their expressions on chart paper.

- **Number of School Days** If you are using the number of school days for Today's Number, and the number is over 100, focus on ways to make 100 using multiples of 5 and 10. For example, if the number is 138, a solution is $25 + 25 + 20 + 20 + 10 + 35 + 3$. Add a card to the class counting strip and fill in another number on the 200 chart.

Activity

Andy the Ant

Display a transparency of Student Sheet 18, Andy the Ant's Paths, on the overhead projector. If the gray line is indistinguishable from the black line, highlight it with a marker.

This is a picture of the ways Andy the Ant walks to school. Andy always walks on the sidewalk. He has three different paths he can follow. He can follow the black line path, the dotted line path, or the gray path [*or name color if it has been highlighted*]. Which path do you think is the longest? How can you tell?

As students share their thinking, ask them to justify how they decided which path is the longest. Some students will visually compare the paths, while others may count blocks or grid lines. Still others may suggest that the path with the greatest number of turns in it (the black line) has to be the longest. Ask these students how they might prove that this path is longer than either of the other two paths.

These paths remind me of the paths we made with paper strips. We found out how long the paths were by counting each strip we used. How can we find out how long these paths are?

If no one suggests using the grid lines, ask how the squares on the paper could help them. Because students may find it hard to articulate counting units on the grid, you might ask them to demonstrate on the overhead.

Distribute Student Sheet 17, Andy the Ant Problems, and Student Sheet 18, Andy the Ant's Paths, to each student.

Today you will be looking at Andy the Ant's paths to school and answering some questions about these paths. You have these things to do: find out which of these three paths to school is the shortest and tell how you know, and decide if there is a shorter path Andy could walk than the paths shown. If you find one, draw it and tell how long the path is. Then, draw the longest path that has two turns and find out how long that path is.

Students can work in pairs, but each student should record on his or her own student sheet.

Observing the Students As students are working, observe the following:

- How do they find the length of each path? Do they count the units accurately?

- How do students plan and draw their new paths? Do they realize that the shortest path will have no turns? How do they figure out the longest path that has only two turns? Do they use trial and error? Or do they think about how far Andy can travel before making one turn, and undoing that turn with the second turn?

Introducing Allison's Travels

Note: Students should complete the Andy the Ant activity before beginning Allison's Travels.

After students finish the Andy the Ant activity, they will have the opportunity to work on three activities during Choice Time. The first of these activities is Allison's Travels. Introduce this activity to the whole class by showing Student Sheet 20, Allison the Ant's Paths, on the overhead projector.

Allison the Ant rides an electric bike around town. She rides to school and to the library. And she rides home. She stays on the roads at all times. Allison's bike runs on a battery. The bike needs its battery charged every 10 blocks. The battery can be charged at home or at a charging station. [*Point out the charging stations.*]

Your job is to show the paths Allison can follow. Remember, she has to charge up her bike battery every 10 blocks.

❖ **Tip for the Linguistically Diverse Classroom** To ensure that students with a limited English proficiency understand the story of Allison the Ant and her electric bike, show students an electric object that uses a battery or a picture of one. Explain how the object depends on a battery to work, as well as how the battery may need to be recharged from time to time. Then compare the battery-run object to Allison's bike in the story.

Distribute Student Sheet 19, Allison the Ant Problems, and Student Sheet 20, Allison the Ant's Paths to each student. Ask students to do problems 1 and 2 on Student Sheet 19 first. For these problems, they draw paths on the grid on Student Sheet 20, Allison the Ant's Paths, then find the length of the paths. Students need to plan the paths so that Allison can stop at a charging station every 10 blocks. Point out that when Allison leaves home, her bike is charged and that each time she leaves a charging station, she has enough power to travel 10 blocks.

Distribute Student Sheets 21 and 22, More Allison the Ant Problems, and More Allison the Ant's Paths. Explain to students that they will solve the problems on Student Sheet 21 by drawing paths on the grid on Student Sheet 22, then find the lengths of the paths. In addition to planning Allison's paths so that her battery can be charged, students will find the length of each path. They can record the lengths next to each path on Student Sheet 22 or next to the problem on Student Sheet 21.

Ask students to put each of these students sheets in their math folders to be completed during Choice Time.

On-Computer Activity: Introducing Tina the Turtle

Tina the Turtle, a computer activity, should also be available for students during Choice Time. Gather students around the demonstration computer. Open *Geo-Logo* and choose Tina the Turtle.

Tina the Turtle rides an electric bike just like Allison the Ant. Like Allison, Tina needs to charge up the bike's battery when its energy runs out. The bike uses energy for every block it travels, and it runs out after 10 blocks, just like Allison's. Let's plan a trip for Tina. Give *Geo-Logo* commands to move her where you want to go.

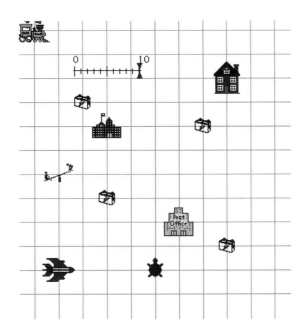

Enter commands that students suggest, without evaluating them in any way. Point out that this activity is different from the Maze game, where the turtle's energy decreased once for every command. For Tina, turns do not use energy, but every step, or block, that Tina travels does use energy. So you have to plan carefully the *length* of your trips.

Explain the following to students:

- All turns are square corner turns, so they are right or left 3 or 6 or 9.
- As they work at the computer, students will record their commands and draw the path on Student Sheet 23, Tina the Turtle Game Commands.
- When their time on the computers is nearly up, students will need to save their work so that they will be able to go on from where they left off during the next session.

You may want to distribute Student Sheet 23 at this time or during Choice Time.

Choice Time

For the remainder of this session and the next one, students will be working with Choice Time activities. Remind them that they need to finish the Making and Comparing Paths activity because you will be discussing it at the end of Session 6.

Post the following list of activities:

> 1. Making and Comparing Paper Paths
>
> 2. Allison's Travels
>
> 3. Tina the Turtle (computer)

For a review of materials and setup and what to watch for during student observations for Choice 1: Making and Comparing Paper Paths, see p. 68.

Choice 2: Allison's Travels

Materials: Students Sheet 19, Allison the Ant Problems, and Student Sheet 20, Allison the Ant's Paths; Student Sheet 21, More Allison the Ant Problems, and Student Sheet 22, More Allison the Ant's Paths.

In this activity, students plan paths that Allison the Ant can follow on her electric bike without running out of power. Problems on Student Sheets 19 and 21 name Allison's starting point and destinations. To solve the problems, students draw paths on the grids shown on the corresponding Student Sheets, 20 and 22. Their paths must allow Allison to stop at a charging station every 10 blocks. They also find the length of Allison's paths.

Choice 3: Tina the Turtle

Materials: Computers with *Geo-Logo* installed; Student Sheet 23, Tina the Turtle Game Commands

Working in pairs at the computer, students open Tina the Turtle and plan trips the turtle can make without running out of energy. Partners take turns entering the commands, switching, for example, about every 5 minutes. The other person writes the commands he or she has entered on the computer on Tina the Turtle Game Commands. Encourage students to refer to the *Geo-Logo* User Sheet posted beside each computer. When the trip is finished, students trace their trip on the grid on Student Sheet 23.

Observing the Students

For observation suggestions for Making and Comparing Paper Paths, refer to p. 68. Use the suggestions given here as a guide for your observations for Choice 2: Allison's Travels, and Choice 3: Tina the Turtle.

Allison's Travels

- How do students plan Allison's route from home to school and back home again? Do they use trial and error?

- Do students plan the route successfully so there is enough energy? Do they find out how far each charging station is from one of Allison's destinations and use that information as they plan her travels?

- What strategies do students use to find the length of the path?

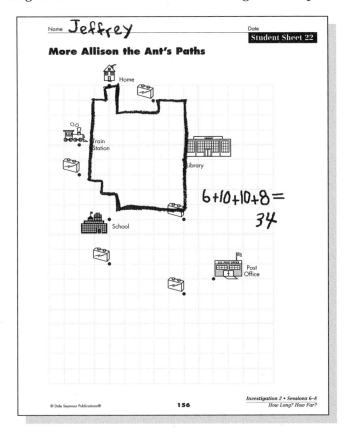

Here is one student's solution for how Allison the Ant travels from home, to the library, to the school, and then home. This student found the total length of the path by adding the distances to each charging station in the path and then recorded a corresponding number sentence next to the grid.

Tina the Turtle

- How do students plan the trips Tina the Turtle makes? Discuss the strategies students use.
- Do students find the total length of the path?
- Do students plan stops at the charging stations? If students need a hint, suggest that they visit a charging station more than once (for example, **b1 f1**) to charge Tina's bike to its limit. Encourage students to change commands if they run out of energy.

Near the End of Each Session   Five or 10 minutes before the end of each choice session, have students stop working, put away materials, and clean up their work areas.

When cleanup is complete, students should record what they worked on during Choice Time in their Weekly Logs.

Activity

Class Discussion: Choice Time Activities

Gather the whole class together to discuss what they did during Choice Time.

Making and Comparing Paper Paths   Ask students to share the lengths of the straight paths and the paths with turns. As students share, ask which path was made of more strips and which had fewer paper strips. Record the number of units in the pairs of paths on the chalkboard.

Paths	
Straight	**Turns**
8	10
5	15
6	14
8	12
6	11

Naomi, Imani, and Lionel said their straight path has 8 paper strips, and their path with turns has 10 strips. Olga, Paul, and Linda made a straight path with 5 paper strips, and a path with turns that has 15 paper strips. And Tory and Chen used 6 paper strips in their straight path and 14 paper strips in their path with turns. What do you notice about the number of strips in the straight paths compared to the number of strips in paths with turns? Think about how many paper strips you used in your straight path and in your path with turns.

Students may notice all the paths with turns used more units. Ask students to talk about why this may be so, encouraging them to see that turns require additional strips.

Ask two pairs or groups of students who built paths between the same two places to describe their paths.

Carla and Lila's straight path from the chalkboard to the windows is 7 paper strips long, and their path with turns is 14 paper strips long. Temara and Graham's straight path to the windows also is 7 strips long, but their path with turns is 12 paper strips long. Why do you think their paths that are straight are the same? Why do you think their paths with turns have different numbers of paper strips?

If students have placed strips correctly, the straight paths between the same points should contain the same number of units. Students may suggest that paths with turns may vary in length because the paths do not start or end at exactly the same point, or because one has more turns.

Allison the Ant Ask students to share their solutions to the Allison the Ant problems. They should describe or show the path and give its length. You may want to have students draw the paths on the overhead. As students share solutions, help them understand that more than one path may be possible. For instance, Allison can travel from home to the library, to school, and back home again in at least two different ways. Then focus on the length of the paths. Is one path longer than another? If so, what makes it longer? Are any paths for a problem the same length? How do those paths compare?

Choosing Student Work to Save

As the unit ends, you may want to use one of the following options for creating a record of students' work.

- Students look back through their folders and write about what they learned in this unit, what they remember most, what was hard or easy for them. You might have students do this work during their writing time.

- Students select one or two pieces of their work as their best work, and you also choose one or two pieces of their work to be saved. This work is saved in a portfolio for the year. Students can create a separate page with brief comments describing each piece of work.

- Send a selection of work home for family members to see. Students write a cover letter, describing their work in this unit. This work should be returned if you are keeping a year-long portfolio of mathematics work for each student.

Sessions 6, 7, and 8 Follow-Up

 **Homework**

Three Paths for Andy the Ant   Students record three different paths Andy the Ant could take to get to Allison the Ant's house on Student Sheet 24, Three Paths for Andy the Ant. They also figure out how long each path is.

Geo-Logo: Shapes and Pictures

What Happens

Students are introduced to Shapes and Pictures, an ongoing activity in which they use *Geo-Logo*'s tools and commands to make shapes and pictures of their own design. Their work focuses on:

- using *Geo-Logo* tools to construct shapes and make pictures
- drawing and measuring paths and turns on the computer

Materials

- Computers with *Geo-Logo* installed

In addition to the *Geo-Logo* games and activities students have worked with in this unit, *Geo-Logo* provides a rich, open-ended environment in which students can explore geometric and measurement concepts. Because students need time to become more proficient writing *Geo-Logo* instructions and using its tools, continue with *Geo-Logo* after this unit. Students will also continue their work with *Geo-Logo* in grade 3.

Shapes and Pictures extends the work with *Geo-Logo*. It introduces students to other *Geo-Logo* commands and tools they can use to make their own pictures and designs. As students construct shapes and create pictures with *Geo-Logo*, they are encouraged to think carefully about properties of shapes, length, and turns and to use geometry-oriented language.

Use a projection device or gather students around a large-screen monitor. Open *Geo-Logo* and choose Shapes and Pictures. Read the directions, then click on **[OK]** or press **<return>**.

Explain that in this activity, students draw shapes such as squares, rectangles, and triangles and pictures of their own design. Introduce some of the frequently used tools. For more information about tools, see Tools in the *Geo-Logo* Teacher Tutorial (p. 116).

Tell students that you are going to teach the turtle to draw a pine tree. Your pine tree will be made of a large green triangle with a small brown trunk.

Activity

On-Computer Activity: Shapes and Pictures

- **First, we'll need to slide the turtle to the left side of the drawing window.** Click on the turtle and drag it to its new location. Keep the turtle oriented to the same direction (0). A jump command is entered in the Command Center. For example, `jump 5 3` would mean jump 5 to the left and 3 up. (Students do not have to know how to interpret these numbers to use this feature.)

- **What color should our pine tree be?** Now we'll click on the Color tool ▣ and then click on a color. **Now the turtle is (green), and when it moves forward, it will make a (green) path.** A set color command is entered in the Command Center.

- **To make a triangle, we have to turn the turtle and then move forward. How far should we turn the turtle?** We can use the Line of Sight tool ▣ or Turtle Turner tool ▣ to help. Click and hold the **Line of Sight tool.** Explain that you would like the turtle to turn from its present direction (indicate the arrow) to the first ray. Enter `r <space> 1 <return>`.

- **Now let's move the turtle forward 10 steps. What command should I enter?** (`f 10`) **Now we have one side of the triangle.**

- **Let's make our triangle have sides that are equal in length. What do we have to do to make the next side?** (Turn, then enter `f 10`.)

- Using the **Line of Sight tool** ▣ or **Turtle Turner tool** ▣ again, explain that you would like the turtle to turn right four turn units; then enter `r 4`. **Now let's move the turtle forward 10.** (Enter `f 10`.)

- **Now we have two equal sides. What do we have to do to make the third side?** (Turn, then enter `f 10`. Repeat previous steps, `r 4` and `f 10`.)

- **Now we have the top of our tree, and we need to make the tree trunk. Let's move the turtle to the middle of the tree.** Click on the turtle and drag it to its new location, just to the left of the midpoint of the bottom of the triangle. The turtle should remain facing the left side of the drawing window. A jump command is again entered in the Command Center.

- **What color should the tree trunk be?** Let's click the Color tool ▣ and click a color. **Now the turtle is (brown), and when it moves forward, it will make a (brown) path.** A set color command is entered in the Command Center.

- **To draw the tree trunk, first we need to turn the turtle.** Use the **Line of Sight tool** ▣ or **Turtle Turner tool** ▣ again to help students determine the size and direction of the turn (`l 3`). Students may find this difficult, due to the turtle's orientation. They can use their Turtle Turners to find the size and direction of the turn, placing the Turtle Turner in the same direction as the turtle on the screen. **Now let's move the turtle forward 2.** (Enter `f 2`.)

- To complete the tree trunk, repeat the commands l 3 and f 2 for each of the two remaining sides. (**Note:** If you wish to hide the turtle, enter the command h t for your final command).

- You may want to show students how to teach the turtle your procedure for drawing a pine tree. For more information, see How to Teach the Turtle Your Procedure (p. 105). **Now we can teach the turtle the procedure for making this tree. I'll click on the Teach tool** [icon]**. (A dialogue box opens.) First, we have to give this procedure a one-word name. What can we name it?** Enter the name students choose in the dialog box. The name and commands are entered in the teach window. Try out the procedure by entering its name in the Command Center.

```
jump x y (x, y are two values)
setc green 2
r 1
f 10
r 4
f 10
r 4
f 10
jump x y
setc brown
l 3
f 2
l 3
f 2
l 3
f 2
ht
```

At this point, you may want to review with students how to save work. Choose **Save My Work** from the **File** menu. When the dialogue box appears, type a name for your work (such as, AG tree 4/17), then click **Save**. (For more detailed information about saving, opening, and printing work, see More About *Geo-Logo*, p. 113.)

You may want to have students plan their shapes and pictures off the computer first. While students are working, discuss any problems they encounter and their solutions. Remind them to use the **Erase One tool** to erase the last command entered, and **<delete>** to change a command previously entered. As students continue to work with Shapes and Pictures or Free Explore, introduce additional tools as they are needed. See p. 116 in the Teacher Tutorial for additional information about tools.

Today's Number

Today's Number is one of the routines that are built into the grade 2 *Investigations* curriculum. Routines provide students with regular practice in important mathematical ideas such as number combinations, counting and estimating data, and concepts of time. For Today's Number, which is done daily (or most days), students write equations that equal the number of days they have been in school. Each day, the class generates ways to make that number. For example, on the tenth day of school, students look for ways to combine numbers and operations to make 10.

This routine gives students an opportunity to explore some important ideas in number. By generating ways to make the number of the day, they explore:

- number composition and part-whole relationships (for example, 10 can be 4 + 6, 5 + 5, or 20 – 10)

- equivalent arithmetical expressions

- different operations

- ways of deriving new numerical expressions by systematically modifying prior ones (for example, 5 + 5 = 10, so 5 + 6 = 11)

Students' strategies evolve over time, becoming more sophisticated as the year progresses. Early in the year, second graders use familiar numbers and combinations, such as 5 + 5 + 10. As they become accustomed to the routine, they begin to see patterns in the combinations and have favorite kinds of number sentences. Later in the year, they draw on their experiences and increased understanding of number. For example, on the forty-ninth day they might include 100 – 51, or even 1000 – 951 in their list of ways to make 49. The types of number sentences that students contribute over time can provide you with a window into their thinking and levels of understanding of number.

If you are doing the full-year grade 2 curriculum, Today's Number is introduced in the first unit, *Mathematical Thinking at Grade 2.* Throughout the curriculum, variations are often introduced as whole-class activities and then carried on in the Start-Up section. The Start-Up section at the beginning of each session offers suggestions for how variations and extensions of Today's Number might be used.

While it is important to do Today's Number every day, it is not necessary to do it during math time. In fact, many teachers have successfully included Today's Number as part of their regular routines at the beginning or end of each day. Other teachers incorporate Today's Number into the odd 10 or 15 minutes that exist before lunch or before a transition time.

If you are teaching an *Investigations* unit for the first time, rather than using the number of days you have been in school as Today's Number, you might choose to use the calendar date. (If today is the sixteenth of the month, 16 is Today's Number.) Or you might choose to begin a counting line that does not correspond to the school day number. Each day, add a number to the strip and use this as Today's Number. Begin with the basic activity and then add variations once students become familiar with this routine.

The basic activity is described below, followed by suggested variations.

Materials

- Chart paper
- Student Sheet 1, Weekly Log
- Interlocking cubes

If you are doing the basic activity, you will also need the following materials:

- Index cards (cut in half and numbered with the days of school so far, for example, 1 through 5 for the first week of school)

- Strips of adding-machine tape

- Blank 200 Charts (tape two blank 100 charts together to form a 10-by-20 grid)

Continued on next page

Basic Activity

Initially, you will want to use Today's Number in a whole group, starting during the first week of school. After a short time, students will be familiar with the routine and be ready to use it independently.

Establishing the Routine

Step 1. Post the chart paper. Call students' attention to the small box on their Weekly Log in which they have been recording the number of days they have been in school.

Step 2. Record Today's Number. Write the number of the day at the top of the chart paper. Ask students to suggest ways of making that total.

Step 3. List the number sentences students suggest. Record their suggestions on chart paper. As you do so, invite the group to confirm each suggestion or discuss any incorrect responses and to explain their thinking. You might have cubes available for students to double-check number sentences.

Step 4. Introduce the class counting strip. Show students the number cards you made and explain that the class is going to create a counting strip. Each day, the number of the day will be added to the row of cards. Post the cards in order in a visible area.

Step 5. Introduce the 200 chart. Display the blank chart and explain that another way the class will keep track of the days in school is by filling in the chart. Record the appropriate numbers in the chart. Tell the class that each day the number of the day will be added to the chart. To help bring attention to landmark numbers on the chart, ask questions such as, "How many more days until the tenth day of school? the twentieth day?"

Variations

When students are familiar with the structure of Today's Number, you can connect it to the number work they are doing in particular units.

Make Today's Number Ask students to use some of the following to represent the number:

- only addition
- only subtraction
- both addition and subtraction
- three numbers
- combinations of 10 ($23 = 4 + 6 + 4 + 6 + 3$ or $23 = 1 + 9 + 2 + 8 + 3$)
- a double ($36 = 18 + 18$ or $36 = 4 + 4 + 5 + 5 + 9 + 9$)
- multiples of 5 and 10 ($52 = 10 + 10 + 10 + 10 + 10 + 2$ or $52 = 5 + 15 + 20 + 10 = 2$)

Use the idea of working backward. Put the number sentences for Today's Number on the board and ask students to determine what number you are expressing: $10 + 3 + 5 + 7 + 5 + 4 = ?$ Notice how students add up this string of numbers. Do they use combinations of 10 or doubles to help them?

In addition to defining how Today's Number is expressed, you can vary how and when the activity is done:

Start the Day with Today's Number Post the day's chart paper ahead of time. When students begin arriving, they can generate number sentences and check them with partners, then record their ways to make the number of the day before school begins. Students can review the list of ways to make the number at that time or at the beginning of math class. At whole group or morning meeting, add the day's number to the 200 chart and the counting strip.

Continued on next page

Choice Time   Post chart paper with the Number of the Day written on it so that it is accessible to students. As one of their choices, students generate number sentences and check them with partners, then record them on the chart paper.

Work with a Partner   Each student works with a partner for 5 to 10 minutes and lists some ways to make the day's number. Partners check each other's work. Pairs bring their lists to the class meeting or sharing time. Students put their lists of number sentences in their math folders. These can be used as a record of students' growth in working with numbers over the school year.

Homework   Assign Today's Number as homework. Students share number sentences sometime during class the following day.

Catch Up   It can be easy to get a few days behind in this routine, so here are two ways to catch up. Post two or three Number-of-the-Day pages for students to visit during Choice Time or free time. Or assign a Number of the Day to individual students. Each can generate number sentences for his or her number, as well as collect number sentences from classmates.

Class History   Post "special messages" below the day's number card to create a timeline about your class. Special messages can include birthdays, teeth lost, field trips, and memorable events, as well as math riddles.

Today's Number Book   Collect the Today's Number charts in a *Number-of-the-Day Book*. Arrange the pages in order, creating chapters based on 10's. Chapter 1, for example, is ways to make the numbers 1 through 10, and combinations for numbers 11–20 become Chapter 2.

How Many Pockets?

How Many Pockets? is one of the classroom routines presented in the grade 2 *Investigations* curriculum. Routines provide students with regular practice in important mathematical ideas such as number combinations, counting and estimating data, and concepts of time. In How Many Pockets? students collect, represent, and interpret numerical data about the number of pockets everyone in the class is wearing on a particular day. This routine often becomes known as Pocket Day. In addition to providing opportunities for comparison of data, Pocket Days provide a meaningful context in which students work purposefully with counting and grouping. Pocket Day experiences contribute to the development of students' number sense—the ability to use numbers flexibly and to see relationships among numbers.

If you are doing the full-year grade 2 *Investigations* curriculum, we suggest you collect pocket data at regular intervals throughout the year. Many teachers collect pocket data every tenth day of school.

The basic activity is described below, followed by suggested variations. Variations are introduced within the context of the *Investigations* units. If you are not doing the full grade 2 curriculum, we suggest you begin with the basic activity and add variations when students become familiar with this routine.

Materials

- Interlocking cubes
- Large jar
- Large rubber band or tape
- Hundred Number Wall Chart and number cards (1–100)
- Pocket Data Chart (teacher made)
- Class list of names
- Chart paper

1	2	3	4	5	6	7	8	9	10
11	12	13	14	15	16	17	18	19	20
21	22	23	24	25	26	27	28	29	30
31	32	33	34	35	36	37	38	39	40
41	42	43	44	45	46	47	48	49	50
51	52	53	54	55	56	57	58	59	60
61	62	63	64	65	66	67	68	69	70
71	72	73	74	75	76	77	78	79	80
81	82	83	84	85	86	87	88	89	90
91	92	93	94	95	96	97	98	99	100

Hundred Number Wall Chart

How many pockets are we wearing today?		
	Pockets	People
Pocket Day 1		

Pocket Data Chart

Basic Activity

Step 1. Students estimate how many pockets the class is wearing today. Students share their estimates and their reasoning. Record the estimates on chart paper. As the Pocket Days continue through the year, students' estimates may be based on the data recorded on past Pocket Days.

Continued on next page

Step 2. Students count their pockets. Each student takes one interlocking cube for each pocket he or she is wearing.

Step 3. Students put the cubes representing their pockets in a large jar. Vary the way in which you do this. For example, rather than passing the jar around the group, call on students with specific numbers of pockets to put their cubes in the jar (for example, students with 3 pockets). Use numeric criteria to determine who puts their cubes in the jar (for example, students with more than 5 but fewer than 8 pockets). Mark the level of cubes on the jar with a rubber band or tape.

Step 4. With students, agree on a way to count the cubes. Count the cubes to find the total number of pockets. Ask students for ideas about how to double-check the count. By re-counting in another way, students see that a group of objects can be counted in more than one way, for example by 1's, 2's, 5's, and 10's. With many experiences, they begin to realize that some ways of counting are more efficient than others and that a group of items can be counted in ways other than by 1, without changing the total.

Primary students are usually most secure counting by 1's, and that is often their method of choice. Experiences with counting and grouping in other ways help them begin to see that number is conserved or remains the same regardless of its arrangement—20 cubes is 20 whether counted by 1's, 2's, or 5's. Students also become more flexible in their ability to use grouping, which is especially important in our number system, in which grouping by 10 is key.

Step 5. Record the total for the day on a Pocket Data Chart. Maintaining a chart of the pocket data as they are accumulated provides natural opportunities for students to see that data can change over time and to compare quantities.

How many pockets are we wearing today?	Pockets	People
Pocket Day 1	41	29

Variations

Comparing Data Students revisit the data from the previous Pocket Day and the corresponding cube level marked on the now empty jar.

On the last Pocket Day, we counted [give number] pockets. Do you think we will be wearing more, fewer, or about the same number of pockets today? Why?

After students explain their reasoning, continue with the basic activity. When the cubes have been collected, invite students to compare the present level of cubes with the previous level indicated by the tape or rubber band and to revise their estimates based on this visual information.

Discuss the revised estimates and then complete the activity. After you add the day's total to the Pocket Data Chart, ask students to compare and interpret the data. To facilitate discussion, build a train of interlocking cubes for today's and the previous Pocket Day's number. As students compare the trains, elicit what the cube trains represent and why they have different numbers of cubes.

Using the Hundred Number Wall Chart Do the basic activity, but this time students choose only one way to count the cubes. Then introduce the Hundred Number Wall Chart as a tool that can be used for counting cubes. This is easiest when done with students sitting on the floor in a circle.

Continued on next page

To check our pocket count, we'll put our cubes in the pockets on the chart. A pocket can have just one cube, so we'll put one cube in number 1's pocket, the next cube in number 2's pocket, and keep going in the same way. How many cubes can we put in the first row?

Students will probably see that 10 cubes will fill the first row of the chart.

One group of 10 cubes fits in this row. What if we complete the second row? How many rows of the chart do you think we will fill with the cubes we counted today?

Encourage students to share their thinking. Then have them count with you and help to place the cubes one by one in the pockets on the chart. When finished, examine the chart together, pointing out the total number of cubes in it and the number of complete rows. For each row, snap together the cubes to make a train of 10. As you do so, use the rows to encourage students to consider combining groups of 10. Record the day's total on the Pocket Data Chart.

Note: If cubes do not fit in the pockets of the chart, place the chart on the floor and place cubes on top of the numbers.

Finding the Most Common Number of Pockets
Each student connects the cubes representing his or her pockets into a train. Before finding the total number of pockets, sort the cube trains with students to find out what is the most common number of pockets. Students pose and investigate additional questions, such as:

- **How many people are wearing the greatest number of pockets?**
- **Is there a number of pockets no one is wearing?**
- **Who has the fewest pockets?**

The cubes are then counted to determine the total number of pockets.

Taking a Closer Look at Pocket Data Each student builds a cube train representing his or her pockets. Beginning with those who have zero pockets, call on students to bring their cube trains to the front of the room. Record the information in a chart, such as the one shown here. You might make a permanent chart with blanks for placing number cards.

_0_ people have 0 pockets.		_0 pockets_
_4_ people have 1 pocket.		_4 pockets_
_2_ people have 2 pockets.		_4 pockets_
_2_ people have 3 pockets.		_6 pockets_

Pose questions about the data, such as, "Two people each have 2 pockets. How many pockets is that?" Then record the number of pockets.

To work with combining groups, you might keep a running total of pockets as data are recorded in the chart until you have found the cumulative total.

We counted 12 (for example) pockets, and then we counted 6 pockets. How many pockets have we counted so far? Be ready to tell us how you thought about it.

As students give their solutions, encourage them to share their mental strategies. Alternatively, after all data have been collected, students can work on the problem of finding the total number of pockets.

Graphing Pocket Data Complete the activity using the Variation, Finding the Most Common Number of Pockets. Leave students' cube trains intact. Each student then creates a representation of the day's pocket data. Provide a variety of materials, including stick-on notes, stickers or paper squares, markers and crayons, drawing paper, and graph paper for students to use.

Continued on next page

These cube trains represent or show how many pockets people are wearing today. Suppose you want to show our pocket data to your family, friends, or students in another classroom. How could you show our pocket data on paper so that someone else could see what we found out about our pockets today?

By creating their own representations, students become more familiar with the data and may begin to develop theories as they consider how to communicate what they know about the data to an audience. Students' representations may not be precise; what's important is that the representations enable them to describe and interpret their data.

Comparing Pocket Data with Another Class
Arrange ahead of time to compare pocket data with a fourth or fifth grade class. Present the following question to students:

Do you think fifth grade students wear more, fewer, or about the same number of pockets as second grade students? Why?

Discuss students' thinking. Then investigate this question by comparing your data with data from another classroom. One way to do this is to invite the other class to participate in your Pocket Day. Do the activity first with the second graders, recording how many people have each number of pockets on the Pocket Data Chart and finding the total number of pockets. Repeat with the other students, recording their data on chart paper. Then compare the two sets of data.

How does the number of pockets in the fifth grade compare to the number of pockets in second grade? Why?

Discuss students' ideas.

Calculate the Total Number of Pockets Divide students into groups of four or five. Each group determines the total number of pockets being worn by the group. Data from each small group are shared and recorded on the board. Using this information, students work in pairs to determine the total number of pockets worn by the class. As a group, they share strategies used for determining the total number of pockets.

In another variation, students share individual pocket data with the group. Each student records this information using a class list of names to keep track. They then determine the total number of pockets worn by the students in the class. Observe how students calculate the total number of pockets. What materials do they use? Do they group familiar numbers together, such as combinations of 10, doubles, or multiples of 5?

Time and Time Again

Time and Time Again is one of the classroom routines included in the grade 2 *Investigations* curriculum. This routine helps second graders develop an understanding of time-related ideas such as sequencing of events, the passage of time, duration of time periods, and identifying important times in their day.

Because many of the ideas and suggestions presented in this routine will be incorporated throughout the school day and into other parts of the curriculum, we encourage teachers to use this routine in whatever way meets the needs of their students and their classroom. We believe that learning about time and understanding ideas about time happen best when activities are presented *over* time and have relevance to students' experiences and lives.

Daily Schedule Post a daily schedule. Identify important times (start of school, math, music, recess, reading) using both analog (clockface) and digital (10:15) representations. Discuss the daily schedule each day and encourage students to compare the actual starting time of, say, math class with what is posted on the schedule.

Talk Time Identify times as you talk with students. For example, "In 15 minutes we will be cleaning up and going to recess." Include specific times and refer to a clock in your classroom, "It's now 10:15. In 15 minutes we will be cleaning up and going out to recess. That will be at 10:30."

Timing One Hour Set a timer to go off at one-hour intervals. Choose a starting time and write both the analog time (using a clockface) and the digital time. When the timer rings, record the time using analog and digital times. At the end of the day, students make observations about the data collected. Initially you'll want to use whole and half hours as your starting points. Gradually you can use times that are 10 or 20 minutes after the hour and also appoint students to be in charge of the timer and of recording the times.

Timing Other Intervals Set a timer to go off at 15-minute intervals over a period of two hours. Begin at the hour and, after the data have been collected, discuss with students what happened each time 15 minutes was added to the time (11:00, 11:15, 11:30, 11:45). You can also try this with 10 minute intervals.

Home Schedule Students make a schedule of important times at home. They can do this both for school days and for nonschool days. They should include both analog and digital times on their schedules. Later in the year they can use this schedule to see if they were really on time for things like dinner, piano lessons, or bedtime. They record the actual time that events happened and calculate how early or late they were. Students can also illustrate their schedules.

Comparing Schedules Partners compare important times in their day, such as what time they eat dinner, go to bed, get up, leave for school. They can compare whether events are earlier or later, and some students might want to calculate how much earlier or later these events occur.

Life Line Students create a timeline of their life. They interview family members and collect information about important developmental milestones such as learning to walk, first word, first day of school, first lost tooth, and important family events. Students then record these events on a life line that is a representation of the first 7 or 8 years of their lives.

Clock Data Students collect data about the types of clocks they have in their home—digital or analog. They make a representation of these data and as a class compare their results.

- **Are there more digital or analog clocks in your house?**

- **Is this true of our class set of data?**

- **How could we compare our individual data to a class set of data?**

Continued on next page

Time Collection Students bring in things from home that have to do with time. Include digital and analog clocks as well as timers of various sorts. These items could be sorted and grouped in different ways. Some students may be interested in investigating different types of time-pieces such as sundials, sand timers, and pendulums.

How Long Is a Minute? As you time 1 minute, students close their eyes and then raise their hands when they think a minute has gone by. Ask "Is a minute longer or shorter than you imagined?" Repeat this activity or have students do this with partners. You can also do this activity with half a minute.

What Can You Do in a Minute? When students are familiar with timing 1 minute, they work in pairs and collect data about things they can do in 1 minute. Brainstorm a list of events that students might try. Some ideas that second graders have suggested include: writing their name, doing jumping jacks or sit-ups, hopping on one foot, saying the ABC's, snapping together interlocking cubes, writing certain numbers or letters (this is great practice for working on reversals), and drawing geometric shapes such as triangles, squares, or stars. Each student chooses four or five activities to do in 1 minute. Before they collect the data, they predict how many they can do. Then with partners they gather the data and compare.

How Long Does It Take? Using a stopwatch or a clock with a second hand, time how long it takes students to complete certain tasks such as lining up, giving out supplies, or cleaning up after math time. Emphasize doing these things in a responsible way. Students can take turns being "timekeepers."

Stopwatches Most second graders are fascinated by stopwatches. You will find that students come up with many ideas about what to time. If possible, acquire a stopwatch for your classroom. (Inexpensive ones are available through educational supply catalogs.) Having stopwatches available in the classroom allows for students teaching each other about time and how to keep track of time.

The following activities will help ensure that this unit is comprehensible to students who are acquiring English as a second language. The suggested approach is based on *The Natural Approach: Language Acquisition in the Classroom* by Stephen D. Krashen and Tracy D. Terrell (Alemany Press, 1983.) The intent is for second-language learners to acquire new vocabulary in an active, meaningful context.

Note that *acquiring* a word is different from *learning* a word. Depending on their level of proficiency, students may be able to comprehend a word upon hearing it during an investigation without being able to say it. Other students may be able to use the word orally but not read or write it. The goal is to help students naturally acquire targeted vocabulary at their present level of proficiency.

We suggest using these activities just before the related investigations. The activities can be led by English-proficient students.

Investigation 1

matching, length, long

1. Display paper strips in varying lengths. Some strips should match others in length. Find two strips that are the same length and tell students that they *match*. Point out that they are the same length. Ask students to find other pairs of paper strips that match.

2. Display all the paper strips again. Point out two paper strips that are different lengths. Tell students that these strips of paper do not match. Ask students to find other pairs of strips that do not match.

3. Ask each student to take a paper strip and find something on themselves that matches it in length, such as their hand, finger, smile, foot, and so on.

farther, farthest, closest, distance

1. As students watch, place objects such as a chalkboard eraser, book, ruler, and pencil at different distances from you.

   Look at the objects I have placed around me. These objects are at different distances from me. The pencil is the closest to me. Which object is the farthest from me?

2. Have a student change the proximity of the objects, so now different objects are closest and farthest.

   Which object is the closest now? Which object is the farthest?

3. Pick up the farthest object and tell students that you are going to place it even *farther* away. Place the object a few feet farther away. Ask a student to pick up another object and place it farther away.

4. Ask students to decide where in the room they could put an object so it is the farthest possible distance from you.

straight, turn, path, left, right

1. Draw three paths on the board. Make path 1 straight, path 2 with two turns, and path 3 with four turns. Ask volunteers to use their fingers to walk along each path.

2. Use your fingers to walk along each path as students use their fingers (in the air) to follow along. Provide a verbal dialogue about the path you are walking.

   Path 1 is a straight path. Let's walk on this path.

   Path 2 is not a straight path. It has 2 turns. [*Indicate the turns.*] Let's walk on this path. First we will walk straight. We will turn to the left, then go straight again. Next we will turn to the right.

   Follow the same procedure for the third path.

3. Have students draw paths from one end of the chalkboard to the other to match your verbal description.

   Draw a straight path. Draw a path with a left turn. Draw a path with a right turn.

   Encourage students to talk about the paths they have drawn.

Teacher Tutorial

Contents

Trouble-Shooting

Geo-Logo Messages

How to Install Geo-Logo on Your Computer

Other Disk Functions

The units in *Investigations in Number, Data, and Space*® ask teachers to think in new ways about mathematics and how students best learn math. Units such as *How Long? How Far?* add another challenge for teachers—to think about how computers might support and enhance mathematical learning. Before you can think about how computers might support learning in your classroom, you need to know what the computer component is, how it works, and how it is designed to be used in the unit. This tutorial is included to help you learn these things.

The tutorial is written for you as an adult learner, as a mathematical explorer, as an educational researcher, as a curriculum designer, and finally—putting all these together—as a classroom teacher. Although it includes parallel (and in some cases the same) investigations as the unit, it is not intended as a walk-through of the student activities in the unit. Rather, it is meant to provide experience using the computer program *Geo-Logo* and to familiarize you with some of the mathematical thinking in the unit.

The tutorial is organized in sessions parallel to the unit. Included in each session are detailed step by step instructions for how to use the computer and the *Geo-Logo* program, along with suggestions for exploring more deeply. The later parts of the tutorial include more detail about each component of *Geo-Logo* and can be used for reference. There is also detailed help available in the *Geo-Logo* program itself.

Geo-Logo is a learning environment designed for mathematical, particularly geometric, exploration. Using *Geo-Logo*, students are able to construct paths and geometric shapes in addition to observing them. Since one of the best ways to learn something is to teach it, *Geo-Logo* uses the metaphor of "teaching the turtle" how to move, turn, and draw. Writing a list of instructions for how to construct a shape encourages students to think carefully about geometric properties and to use geometry-oriented language.

Teachers new to using computers and *Geo-Logo* can follow the detailed step by step instructions. Those with more experience might not need to read each step. As is true with learning any new approach or tool, you will test out hypotheses, make mistakes, be temporarily stumped, go down wrong paths, and so on. This is part of learning, but may be doubly frustrating because you are dealing with computers. It might be helpful to work through the tutorial and the unit in parallel with another teacher. If you get particularly frustrated, ask for help from the school computer coordinator or another teacher more familiar with using computers. It is not necessary to complete the tutorial before beginning to teach the unit. You can work through in parts, as you prepare for parallel investigations in the unit.

Although the tutorial will help prepare you for teaching the unit, you will learn most about *Geo-Logo* and how it supports the unit as you work side by side with your students.

Note: These directions assume that *Geo-Logo* has been installed on the hard drive of your computer. If it has not, see How to Install *Geo-Logo* on Your Computer, p. 129.

☞ 1. Turn on the computer by doing the following:

  a. If you are using an electrical power surge protector, switch to the ON position.

  b. Switch the computer (and the monitor, if separate) to the ON position.

  c. Wait until the desktop or workspace appears.

☞ 2. Open *Geo-Logo* by doing the following:

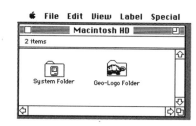

  a. Double-click on the *Geo-Logo* folder icon if it is not already open. To double-click, click twice in rapid succession without moving the pointer.

  b. Double-click on the *Geo-Logo* icon in this folder.

  c. Wait until the *Geo-Logo* opening screen appears. Single-click on this screen when the message appears.

Depending on your computer, you may see things on the screen in addition to or behind the *Geo-Logo* windows. These are other computer functions that may be available to you but are not part of *Geo-Logo*. If you click one of these by mistake, you can return to *Geo-Logo* by clicking into any *Geo-Logo* window or selecting it from the desktop. For additional information, see Trouble-Shooting, p. 125.

Start an activity by doing the following:

☞ 1. Single-click on the **Steps** activity (or on any activity you want to start).

How to Start an Activity

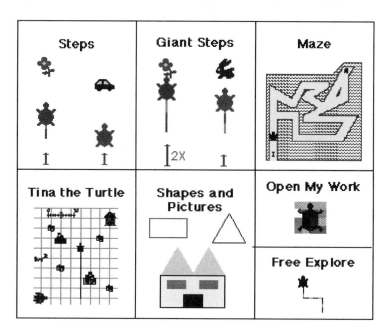

When you choose an activity, the Tool window, Command Center, Drawing window, and Teach window for that activity fill the screen.

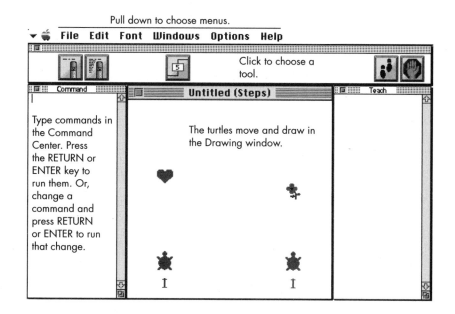

A dialogue box appears with directions.

> **Players take turns clicking on their turtle, then entering an 'f' command to get their turtle to their goal.**
>
> [OK]

 2. Click on **[OK]** or press **<return>** to close the dialogue box.

Should you need them, trouble-shooting notes are included on page 125.

How to Do the Steps Activity

The turtles in *Geo-Logo* are robots that follow your commands. The object of Steps is to write as few commands as possible for the turtle to follow so it reaches the target object. You will estimate distances and use the command **f** for forward.

 1. Enter commands in the Command Center to make the turtle go from where it starts to the target picture directly ahead of it.

    a. Type **f 5 (f <space> 5)**.

       Use **<delete>** to make changes, if needed. If the text you type does not appear in the Command Center, click somewhere in the Command Center to make it the "active" window—the one that receives text.

    b. Press **<return>**.

       The turtle moves forward 5 steps. The length of each step is shown on the screen below the turtle.

       Typing a command and pressing **<return>** to run it is called *entering* a command.

 2. Make the *second* turtle go from where it starts to the target picture directly ahead of it.

    a. Click on the turtle at the right; this is turtle2. A "talkto" command was automatically entered in the Command Center. All commands will now be directed to turtle2.

    b. Enter a forward **f** command.

 3. Continue until both turtles reach their targets.

    a. Continue to enter forward commands, clicking on the turtles as needed. When the turtle lands directly on the target, the target grows and shrinks to show it has been reached.

b. If you overshoot a target, click on the **Erase One tool** in the tool bar at the top of the screen. It erases the last command entered. Or use the back command (e.g., b 2). You can also use **<delete>** to erase a number and change it.

c. Sometimes a number entered is so large that the turtle goes off the screen. When this happens, use either the **Erase One tool** to erase the command, press **<delete>** to change the number to a smaller number, or enter a back b command.

d. You may be working with a partner who clicked on the turtle, so you can't click on yours (because it's still off the screen). You can go up and change your last command or enter t1, or t2, (with the comma), which are short for talkto turtle1 and talkto turtle2.

4. Click on the **Erase All tool** to clear the Command Center and place new targets in new locations. Repeat the activity as you like.

The turtle is a robot that follows certain *Geo-Logo* commands. If it does not understand a command, it will write a message in a dialogue box. See the section *Geo-Logo* Messages, p. 127.

To edit (change) your commands, use **<delete>** to back over and erase text. Type new text and press **<return>**. Or use the mouse to select words or blocks of text by dragging (pressing and holding down the mouse button as you move the mouse) over the text. Then press **<delete>** and type new text.

Each time you change a command and press **<return>**, the turtle reruns the commands.

More About Steps

Remember that assistance is available from the **Help** menu at any time: Choose **Windows**, **Vocabulary** (Commands), **Tools**, **Directions**, or **Hints**.

The Tool window for Steps:

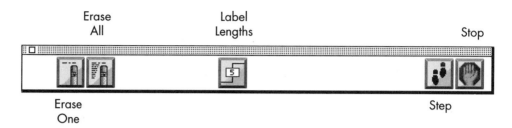

	Icon		Description
	Erase One		Erases the last command run.
	Erase All		Erases all the commands in the Command Center.
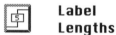	**Label Lengths**		Used to show length of line segments, in turtle steps, on the Drawing window.
	Step		Used to show and follow one command at a time in either the Command Center or in a procedure to help find errors and edit.
	Stop		Stops commands that are running.

■ For more details about these and other tools, see Tools, p. 116

How to Label the Measures of Your Paths

It may be helpful to see the measures of each line segment made by a forward or back command. For example, this might help you figure out how to get to the target with a single command. *Geo-Logo* has tools to help you think about these measures.

■ You can label the lengths of line segments in your path.

■ Click on the **Label Lengths tool** to turn on the labeling.

The line segments in the path, made by a forward or back command, are labeled with their lengths.

■ Click on the **Label Lengths tool** again to turn off the labeling.

☞ 1. Finish working on this activity:

   If you want to have students save their work, students choose **Close My Work** from the **File** menu. A dialogue box may appear asking whether you wish to save your work.

   Notice that the computer is ready to start new work on this activity. If others will be doing the same activity, you may want to leave the screen like this instead of quitting *Geo-Logo* and shutting down the computer.

☞ 2. To finish using *Geo-Logo:*

   Choose **Quit** from the **File** menu.

☞ 3. To finish using the computer:

   a. Follow the usual procedure to shut down and turn off your computer.

How to Finish an Activity

How to Choose a New Activity

☞ 1. Choose **Change Activity** from the **File** menu.

A dialogue box may appear asking whether you wish to save your work. For now, click [Don't Save].

☞ 2. Single-click on the new activity button on the *Geo-Logo* activities screen.

How to Play Giant Steps

Choose **Change Activity** from the **File** menu. Click on the Giant Steps activity. A dialogue box appears with directions.

```
Players take turns clicking on their
turtle, then entering an 'f' command to
get their turtle to their goal.

                                    [  OK  ]
```

As in Steps, the goal is to get your turtle to the target with the fewest possible commands. In Giant Steps, however, one unit length of one turtle is double or triple the other's. This relationship is indicated by the number next to the larger unit. Also, in Giant Steps the targets are always the same distance away (so that you are encouraged to use that relationship).

☞ 1. Click on the turtle whose unit length is 2 or 3 times the other's unit length.

☞ 2. Enter commands in the Command Center to make the turtle go from where it starts to the target picture directly ahead of it.

☞ 3. Click on the turtle whose unit length is the small unit.

☞ 4. Enter commands in the Command Center to make the turtle go from where it starts to the target picture directly ahead of it. Use the multiplicative relationship to do it with a single command. That is, if it took you 6 steps to get to the target with a unit length 2 times as long, try f 12.

☞ 5. Click on the **Erase All tool** to clear the Command Center and place new targets in new locations.

☛ 1. Choose **Change Activity** from the **File** menu. Click on the Maze activity. A dialogue box appears with directions.

How to Begin a Maze

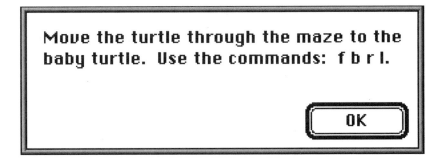

Move the turtle through the maze to the
baby turtle. Use the commands: f b r l.

OK

☛ 2. After you read the directions, click on **[OK]** or press **<return>** to close the dialogue box.

A window appears, set up for the Maze activity.

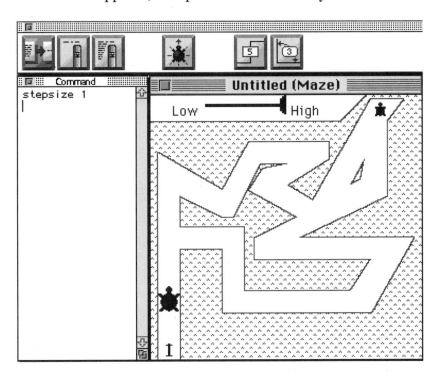

The goal is to write commands that will rescue the baby turtle who is lost in the maze. The stepsize of the turtle is indicated both by the `stepsize 1` command in the Command Center and by the line segment behind the adult turtle. (The stepsize might be 2 or 3. If you want it to be 1, just change the number to 1 in the Command Center and press **<return>**.) Besides moving with the **f** and **b** commands, you need to turn the turtle.

Entering r and a number turns the turtle that number of units to the right; entering l and a number turns the turtle that number of units to the left.

r 3   right turn 3 units   turns the turtle 3 units, as if from 12 to 3 o'clock (i.e., right 90 degrees)

l 5   left turn 5 units   turns the turtle 5 units, as if from 12 to 7 o'clock (i.e., left 150 degrees)

How to Complete the Maze

☞ 1. Enter commands in the Command Center to make the turtle go through the maze. For example:

a. Enter f 6 (f **<space>** 6) [if you picked a different stepsize, this number would be less].

Notice that each command you give uses one bit of energy. The energy is limited to encourage you to use the fewest and most efficient commands.

b. Enter r 3.

Notice that the turtle rotates 90° on its belly to make a right turn. Turn rays are displayed to show the rotation.

c. Continue to type commands to make the turtle rescue the baby turtle.

☞ 2. Check to see if you can combine any commands to use less battery energy.

To make changes, move up or down with the mouse or arrow keys, use **<delete>** to erase, and type in your change. After you finish all your changes, press **<return>**. You will see the effect of these changes in the Drawing window. For example, if you entered f 2 f 2 f 2, you could change these to one command, f 6, to save energy.

Some of the tasks involve the measures of the path. *Geo-Logo* has tools that help you to think about these measures. The **Label Lengths tool** has already been described. You can also label the measures of turns.

You can label the measures of turns in your path.

■ Click on the **Label Turns tool** to turn on the labeling.

The measure of each turn is labeled.

■ Click on the **Label Turns tool** again to turn off the labeling.

How to Label the Measures of Your Turns

☞ 1. Check to see if your procedure draws the path you want.

To make changes, move up or down with the mouse or arrow keys, use the delete key to erase, and type in your change. After you finish all your changes, press **<return>** and you will see the effect of these changes in the Drawing window.

☞ 2. Teach the turtle your new procedure to travel through the maze by following these steps:

a. Click on the **Teach tool** .

This defines the list of commands in the Command Center as a procedure. The computer will ask you to type a name for the procedure.

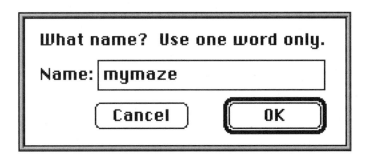

What name? Use one word only.

Name: mymaze

Cancel   OK

b. Type a one-word name for this procedure, such as **mymaze**. You can use letters or numbers.

c. Click **[OK]** or press **<return>**.

The procedure appears in the Teach window. It is defined by the name you give it. Notice that the computer adds a first and a last line to your commands. The first line is "**to mymaze**" (or whatever name you chose), and the last line is **end**.

How to Teach the Turtle Your Procedure

The drawing window clears in preparation for your next entry.

You have taught the turtle to solve the maze.

☞ 3. Run your procedure by following these steps.

    a. For the Maze activity (only), you first have to delete the stepsize command by placing your cursor at the end of the command and repeatedly pressing **\<delete\>**.

    If needed, first move the text cursor (the blinking vertical line that shows where any typed text will go) into the Command Center by clicking the mouse in that window.

    b. Type your procedure's name, for example, **mymaze**, in the Command Center.

    c. Press **\<return\>**.

If you want to make changes to your procedure, you may edit any commands in the Teach window. Click your cursor in that window, move up or down with the mouse or arrow keys, use **\<delete\>** to erase, and type in your changes. When you click out of that window, the turtle will rerun your procedure to show your changes.

☞ 1. Choose **Change Activity** from the **File** menu. Click on the Tina the Turtle activity. A dialogue box appears with directions.

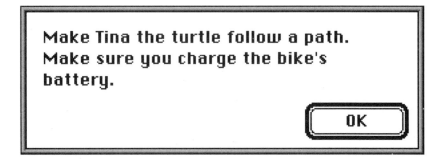

☞ 2. After you read the directions, click on **[OK]** or press **<return>** to close the dialogue box.

The usual window appears, set up for the Tina the Turtle activity.

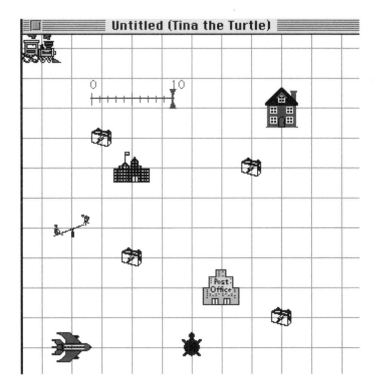

Tina visits locations on her electric bike. Tina needs to charge up the bike's battery when its energy gets low. The bike uses energy for every block it travels. That is, unlike the Maze activity, in this activity it is the distance traveled that uses energy.

How to Complete Tina the Turtle

☞ 1. Enter commands in the Command Center to make the turtle go through the streets of the Tina the Turtle activity to the school. After each command, press **<return>**.

   a. Enter **f 6** (f **<space>** 6).

   Each step of Tina's uses one bit of energy. The command **f 6** uses six times as much energy as the command **f 1**.

   b. Enter **l 3**.

   Notice that turns do not use energy. Energy used is equal to the number of steps—that is, the number of blocks traveled.

   The turns in this activity are all square corner turns, so they are right or left 3 (or 6 or 9).

   c. Enter **f 2**.

   Animation shows that you reached the school.

☞ 2. Give commands that will take Tina to a battery.

   a. Enter **f 1**.

   You receive a notice that your energy is getting low.

   b. Enter **r 3 f 1**.

   You reach a battery charger and your energy increases.

☞ 3. Give commands that take Tina to other locations. Plan the distances of each trip so that you do not run out of energy.

Free Explore

The Free Explore activity is available for you to use to extend and enhance activities in the unit and as an environment to further explore mathematics with *Geo-Logo*. Develop your own ideas and projects.

In Free Explore, the turtle responds to all *Geo-Logo* commands, and all tools are available from the tool bar.

The following features of *Geo-Logo* will be especially helpful to your students.

About Free Explore

See complete descriptions of these and other tools beginning on p. 116. These tools are particularly useful here.

Tools

- The **Ruler tool** ▦ measures lengths, and the **Line of Sight tool** ▦ or **Turtle Turner tool** ▦ measures turns.

- The **Color tool** ▦ sets the turtle's pen color; you choose one of the colors on the color tools bar.

- The **Step tool** ▦ can be used to "walk through" commands in the Command Center or in a procedure. This is useful for debugging, or finding mistakes.

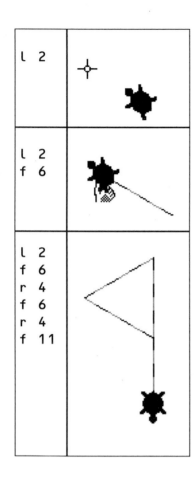

- The **Draw Commands tool** allows you to use the mouse to turn and move the turtle directly as corresponding *Geo-Logo* commands are created automatically and written in the Command Center.

    a. Click on the **Draw Commands tool**.

    Notice that when you move the cursor into the Drawing window, it changes into cross-hairs and the turtle turns to face it. As you move it with the mouse, the turtle continually turns to face in that direction and a corresponding turn command is written and updated in the Command Center.

    b. Move the cross-hairs in the desired direction.

    c. Click to freeze and accept a turn command for the turtle.

    Notice that the cursor now changes into a hand that can be used to move the turtle along a path in the chosen direction.

    d. Drag the turtle to the next location. You can drag it only in the direction in which it is heading.

    e. Release the mouse button to freeze and accept a move command for the turtle.

    f. Continue to create new turn and move commands to complete your drawing.

    g. Click in any other window—for example, the Command Center—to stop using this tool.

- The **Scale tool** allows you to use the mouse to change the size of a figure on the Drawing window.

Make sure a pattern of f and r (or l) commands have been run in the Command Center.

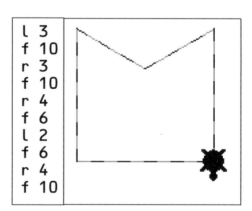

Use the Scale tool to change the size of your drawing, keeping its shape the same.

Click on the **Scale tool**.
The cursor changes to a
hand. Click on your figure
with the cursor.

```
l  3
f  10
r  3
f  10
r  4
f  6
l  2
f  6
r  4
f  10
```

Drag a corner or side.
Notice that the **f** commands
change in proportion, but
the turn commands remain
the same. Release the mouse
button when you are done.

```
l  3
f  5
r  3
f  5
r  4
f  3
l  2
f  3
r  4
f  5
```

■ The **Change Shape tool** is available *only* if you set two items in the
Options menu: (1) **Turn in Degrees** must be checked, and (2) **Scale
Distance...** must be set to 1.

Make sure a pattern of **f**
and **r** (or **l**) commands have
been run in the Command
Center. This tool is available
only if turns are in degrees.

```
l  3
f  5
r  3
f  5
r  4
f  3
l  2
f  3
r  4
f  5
```

Click on the **Change Shape tool**.

a. The turtle disappears. To move the top right line segment, click anywhere on the segment and drag it to down to its new location. The commands change automatically. Release the mouse button when you are done.

Commands	
l 90	
f 5	
r 90	
f 5	
r 30	
f 5	
r 31	
f 3	
r 120	
f 11	

b. Drag a corner to the new location. The commands change automatically. Release the mouse button when you are done.

c. Keep dragging corners or sides to get the best approximation you can.

d. Click in the Command Center to stop using the tool.

Commands	
l 90	
f 5	
r 90	
f 5	
r 90	
f 4	
l 77	
f 6	
r 167	
f 11	

Note: To use the Scaling and Change Shape tools, the Command window must have a pattern of only f and r (or l) commands.

Help

Assistance is available as you work with *Geo-Logo* activities. From the **Help** menu, choose any of the following:

Windows provides information on *Geo-Logo*'s three main windows: Command Center, Drawing, and Teach.

Vocabulary provides a listing of *Geo-Logo*'s commands and examples.

Tools provides information on *Geo-Logo*'s tools (represented on the Tools window as icons).

Directions provides instructions for the present activity.

Hints gives a series of hints on the present activity, one at a time. It is dimmed when there are no available hints.

How to Save Your Work

When you turn off the computer or start a new activity, the computer's memory is cleared of all commands and procedures to make room for new ones. To avoid losing your work, you can save it on a disk before the computer memory is cleared. Once your work has been saved on a disk, you can open it again to show it to someone or to work on it some more.

☞ 1. Choose **Save My Work** from the **File** menu:

    a. Move the mouse pointer over the word **File** in the menu title bar along the top of the screen.

    b. Press and hold the mouse button until the menu items appear.

    c. Continue to press the mouse button as you drag the pointer down and select **Save My Work**.

    d. Release the mouse button.

    (To save using the keyboard, hold down **<⌘>** and type **<s>**.)

The first time you save your work, a dialogue box, such as the following, will appear asking for a name.

File

New Work	⌘N
Open My Work...	⌘O
Close My Work	⌘W
Save My Work	**⌘S**
Save My Work As...	
Change Activity...	
Load Window...	
Save Window As...	
Page Setup	
Print	⌘P
Print Window	
Quit	⌘Q

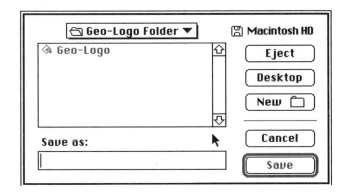

☞ 2. Type a name for your work, such as JS Maze 11/22. (You can choose any name for a program. However, useful program names include information that helps you find them again, such as the person, activity, and date. Spaces can be used in the titles of saved work.) You can also choose a different location for your work. The bar with the name "*Geo-Logo* Folder" tells where the work will be saved. It also is a pop-up menu that can be used to change the folder into which you can save your work.

☞ 3. Click on **[Save]**.

Notice that the name of your work now appears in the title bar of the Drawing window.

When you save your work this way, a copy is stored on the computer disk. You can stop using the computer for a while or come back to this work at another time.

How to Continue with Saved Work

☞ 1. To continue with your previous work:

a. If you are starting your computer, open *Geo-Logo*, and click on **Open My Work** in the activity window.

or

b. Choose **Open My Work** from the **File** menu.
In either case, a dialogue box opens.

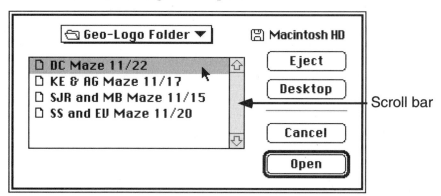

Scroll bar

If your work has been saved on a different disk, insert that disk, click **[Desktop]**, and choose that disk from the menu.

c. Select work by clicking on its title in the list. You may need to scroll up and down the list to find your title. Click on the up or down arrows in the scroll bar.

d. Click on **[Open]** (or double-click on the title).

- Choose **Show Notes** from the **Windows** menu to record thoughts and observations about your work. (See example below.) To close Notes, choose **Hide Notes** from the **Windows** menu or click in the close box on the left side of the Notes title bar.

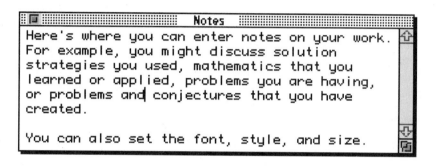

- You can print all your work including the picture and list of commands and procedures. Choose **Print** from the **File** menu.

- You can print a single window if you want only a list of your commands, or a copy of your picture or notes. Click into that window and choose **Print Window** from the **File** menu.

- You can enlarge all the letters in the Command Center and Teach window for easier viewing. Select **All Large** from the **Font** menu. Select **All Small** to change back to the normal font size.

How to Make Notes and Print Work

Tools

Only the most commonly used tools are available and displayed for each activity. All tools are available in Free Explore.

Click on a tool to use it.

Teach

Teaches the turtle your procedure. Give the procedure a name. Enter its name in the Command Center to run it.

Ruler

Move the cursor to a point on the Drawing window. Click to find the length from the turtle to that point.

Line of Sight

Click and hold the mouse button to see a turtle turner show the turtle's heading.

Turtle Turner

Move the cursor on the Drawing window to turn the arrow. Click to show the turn command.

Draw Commands

Move the pointer and click to create a turn command. Then grab the turtle and pull it forward or back.

Change Shape

Click on a line segment or corner and drag it to its new location.

Grid

Puts a grid on the Drawing window, or removes it.

Erase One

Takes away the last command run.

Erase All

Erases all commands in the Command Center.

Label Lengths

Labels the lengths of all line segments.

Label Turns

Labels the amount of each turtle turn.

Scale

Click on a line segment or corner and drag to change the size—but not the shape—of the figure.

Colors

After the tools change to colors, click the color you want.

Step

Steps through a procedure in the Command Center or Teach window. Click on the Drawing window to run each command. If you wish to stop, click on another window.

Stop

Stops all commands.

 Teach

Teaches the turtle a procedure, defined by the sequence of commands in the Command Center. You are asked to provide the name of the new procedure. The name and the commands are then placed in the Teach window. You can then enter its name in the Command Center to run the procedure. If you wish to change the procedure, you can edit it in the Teach window. If the procedure is in the Command Center, the change will be reflected in the Drawing window as soon as you click out of the Teach window.

 Erase One

Erases the last command typed or run.

 Erase All

Erases all the commands in the Command Center.

Measures length, starting at the turtle's position. The other end of the ruler follows the cursor that you move with the mouse. Click to freeze the ruler and show the length in a dialogue box.

 Ruler

Draws an arrow to show the turtle's heading and rays for each 30°.

 Line of Sight

Measures turns from the turtle's heading. One arrowhead shows the turtle's heading. The other follows the cursor, which you move with the mouse. Click to freeze this arrowhead and show a turn command.

 Turtle Turner

Used to show length of line segments, in turtle steps, on the Drawing window.

 Label Lengths

Used to show the amount of each turtle turn, in degrees, on the Drawing window.

 Label Turns

Enables you to use the mouse to turn and move the turtle, with corresponding *Geo-Logo* commands created automatically. You continuously create first a turn (r or l) command, then a movement (f or b) command.

 Draw Commands

First, the turtle turns to face the cursor, which you move with the mouse. The corresponding turn command is continuously updated in the Command Center. Click to freeze the turtle.

Second, click on and drag the turtle forward or back (a dotted box shows each new location). Release the mouse button to move the turtle to that position and place the corresponding f or b command in the Command Center.

Available only if you set two items in the **Options** menu: (1) **Turn in Degrees** (must be checked) and (2) **Scale Distance...** must be set to 1. Allows you to use the mouse to change the shape of a figure on the Drawing window. All commands in the Command Center must be in a simple f _ r _ b _ r _... pattern. When you click on the tool, the turtle disappears. Click anywhere on a line segment or corner and drag it to a new location. The corresponding commands in the Command Center are changed automatically.

 Change Shape

Scale

Allows you to use the mouse to change the size of a figure on the Drawing window. All commands in the Command Center must be in a simple f __ r __ f __ r __... pattern. When you click on the tool, the turtle disappears. Click anywhere on the figure and drag it toward or away from the center of the screen (the turtle's "home"). The figure becomes larger or smaller and the corresponding commands in the Command Center are changed automatically.

 Colors

Changes the tools bar to a selection of colors. Click one color to automatically change the turtle's color.

 Grid

Places a dot grid on the Drawing window, or removes the grid if it is present.

 Step

Allows you to step through the commands one at a time, in the Command Center or in a procedure in the Teach window. Click in the Drawing window. One command at a time is highlighted and run. To stop and change a command, click outside of the Drawing window.

 Stop

Stops commands that are running.

Motions

Examples of Motions

The following motion is automatically available in Free Explore.

Move Turtle   To move the turtle, click on the turtle and drag it by pressing and holding the mouse button while you move the mouse.

A jumpto command is automatically placed in the Command Center.

Click . . .   . . . then drag to move the turtle.

You can slide and turn any procedure that has been defined in the Teach window.

Slide To slide a procedure, click in the middle of one of its *line segments* and drag it to a new location. Release the mouse button when the procedure is in the correct location.

Click here . . .   . . . and this   Then drag
                         cursor appears.   the shape.

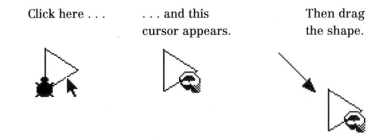

A s l i d e command is automatically placed in the Command Center.

Turn Hold the shift key down and click on a shape. Drag it in a circle to turn the procedure. Release the mouse button when the procedure has the desired orientation.

Hold the shift   . . . and this   Then drag to
key and click . .   cursor appears.   turn the shape.

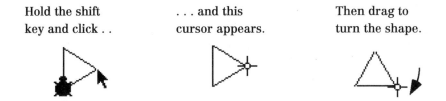

A t u r n i t command is automatically placed in the Command Center (in the example above, t u r n i t r 3).

Note: You cannot drag the corner at which the turtle starts drawing the procedure, because that is the point around which the procedure turns.

Commands

The following commands are available in *Geo-Logo*. Some have been previously introduced in the investigations where they are most useful. You can see all of *Geo-Logo*'s commands by selecting **Vocabulary** from the **Help** menu.

Command	What It Means	What It Does
b 10	back 10	Moves the turtle back 10 steps (use whatever number you wish). The turtle leaves a path if its pen is down. You can use b k as well. *See also* pd *and* pu.
ct	clear text	Clears, or erases, all the text in the Print window.
f 5	forward 5	Moves the turtle forward 5 steps (use whatever number you wish). You can use f d as well. *See also* pd *and* pu.
fill	fill	Fills a closed shape or the entire Drawing window with the current turtle's color, starting at the current turtle's position. If the turtle's pen is over a path, only that path is filled. To fill a shape, use pu, then f and r or l to move inside the shape. Use setc to set the color, then fill. **Note:** If the shape you want to fill is on a grid, turn off the grid before filling. Use the hp command to hide points if you want to use jumpto or motions with fill.
ht	hide turtle	Hides the current turtle (it becomes invisible).
jump −3 1	jump	Moves the turtle three steps to the left and one step up.
l 3	left 3	Turns the turtle left 3 turn units (as if a clock hand turned from 4 to 1; equal to 90 degrees).
pd	pen down	Puts the turtle's pen down so that when it moves, it draws a path.
print [My drawing.]		Prints whatever is in brackets (or a word, or number) in the Print window. Can be used as a calculator. If you type pr 85 + 15, *Geo-Logo* will print 100. Can be abbreviated "pr."
print colors		Prints a list of colors to use with the setc command.
pu	pen up	Puts the turtle's pen up so that when it moves, it does not draw a path.
recycle		Cleans up and reorganizes available memory.
repeat 4 [f 10 r 90]		Repeats the commands in the list the specified number of times; in this example, 4 times. (The list is whatever is between the [square brackets].)
r 4	right 4	Turns the turtle right 4 turn units (as if a clock hand turned from 1 to 5; equal to 120 degrees).
rt 30	right 30 degrees	Turns the turtle right 30 degrees.
setc black	set color	Sets the turtle's color; this affects the color of the turtle and the color for drawing and filling. The color names are: white black gray gray2 yellow orange red pink violet blue blue2 green green2 brown brown2 gray3.
st	show turtle	Shows the turtle.

How to Use Menus

To use any menu, do the following:

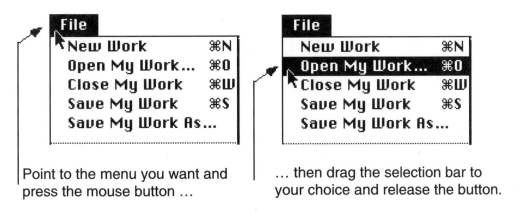

Point to the menu you want and press the mouse button ...

... then drag the selection bar to your choice and release the button.

Some menu choices are also available from the keyboard. On the menu, the ⌘ N indicates that, instead of selecting the choice from the menu, you could type ⌘ N. Hold down the Command key (with the ⌘ and symbols on it), then press **<N>**.

A menu choice may be dimmed, indicating it is not available in a particular situation.

Geo-Logo's Menus

The **File** menu deals with documents and quitting.

> **New Work** starts a new document.
>
> **Open My Work...** opens previously saved work.
>
> **Close My Work** closes present work.
>
> **Save My Work** saves the work.
>
> **Save My Work As...** saves the work with a new name to a different disk or folder.
>
> **Change Activity...** shows the activity screen to allow you to select a new activity.
>
> **Load Window...** allows you to select a text file to load into a window.
>
> **Save Window As...** saves a window as a text file.
>
> **Page Setup** brings up a dialogue box to set up the page for printing.
>
> **Print** prints a whole document.
>
> **Print Window** prints only the active window (the last one clicked on).
>
> **Quit** quits *Geo-Logo*.

File	Edit	Font	Windo
New Work			⌘N
Open My Work...			⌘O
Close My Work			⌘W
Save My Work			⌘S
Save My Work As...			
Change Activity...			
Load Window...			
Save Window As...			
Page Setup			
Print			⌘P
Print Window			
Quit			⌘Q

Edit

Undo	⌘Z
Cut	⌘H
Copy	⌘C
Paste	⌘U
Clear	
Stopall	⌘.

The **Edit** menu contains choices to use when editing your work:

Undo reverses the last thing done, such as delete, cut, paste, erase, or erase all.

Cut deletes the selected object and saves it to a space called the clipboard.

Copy copies selected object to the clipboard.

Paste places the contents of the clipboard in the cursor location.

Clear deletes the selected object (works the same as using **<delete>**).

Stopall stops running the procedure.

Font

Chicago
Courier
Geneva
Helvetica
Monaco
New York
Times
Other ▶

Size ▶
Style ▶

All Large

The **Font** menu is used to change the appearance of text. The change applies to the active window (the Command Center, Teach, Print, or Notes windows).

The first names are choices of typeface.

Size and **Style** have additional choices; pull down to select them and then to the right. See the example for **Style** shown at left. The **Size** choice works the same way.

All Large changes all text in all windows to a large-size font. This is useful for demonstrations. This selection toggles (changes back and forth) between **All Large** and **All Small**.

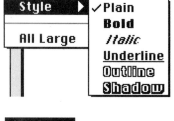

Windows

Hide Command Center
Hide Drawing
Hide Teach
Hide Tools

Show Print
Show Notes

The **Windows** menu shows or hides the windows. If you hide a window, such as the Drawing window, the menu item changes to **Show** followed by the name of the window—for example, **Show Drawing**. You can also hide a window by clicking in the "close box" in the upper-left-hand corner of the window.

The **Show Print** choice opens the Print window and displays text generated by a print command from the Command Center. The **Notes** choice opens and hides the Notes window. You can use this window to enter and keep permanent notes.

The **Options** menu allows you to customize *Geo-Logo*.

> **Fast Turtle** turns the turtle quickly and so speeds up drawing. Usually in *Geo-Logo*, the turtle turns slowly to help students build images of the turns.
>
> **Turn Rays** displays rays during turns to help students visualize the turn. After a turn command is entered, a ray is drawn to show the turtle's initial heading. Then as the turtle turns, another ray turns with it, showing the change in heading throughout the turn. A ray also marks every 30° of turn.
>
> **Counting** displays (with alternating colors) and counts the steps the turtle takes in drawing a figure. Uncheck this option in Free Explore to draw with solid lines and turn off the counting feature.
>
> **Scale Distance...** controls units of measure for distance. If you enter 10 in the top left-hand box, the turtle will go forward 10 of the usual turtle steps when the command f 1 is entered. If the "1 cm" or "1 inch" button is clicked, the proper number of steps is automatically entered; for instance, 72 for "1 inch." In this example, the command f 1 would move the turtle 1 inch on the screen. Note that this also encourages students to use fractions and decimals in issuing commands.
>
> **Turn in Degrees** changes the unit of rotation to degrees. If it is not checked, as shown here, the unit of rotation is the usual "turn unit" (30°, or "clock turns").

Note: These options can be used together to set *Geo-Logo*'s turtle to run as most turtles do.

1. **Fast Turtle** should be checked.
2. **Turn Rays** should be checked (or unchecked to turn off).
3. **Count** should be checked (or unchecked to turn off).
4. **Scale Distance...** should be set to 1.
5. **Turn in Degrees** should be checked.

The **Help** menu provides assistance.

> **Windows...** provides information on *Geo-Logo*'s three main windows: Command Center, Drawing, and Teach.
>
> **Vocabulary...** provides a dictionary of *Geo-Logo*'s commands and examples of their use.
>
> **Tools...** provides information on *Geo-Logo*'s tools (represented on the Tools window as icons).
>
> **Directions...** provides instructions for the present activity.
>
> **Hints...** gives a series of hints on the present activity, one at a time. It is dimmed when there are no available hints.

```
Options   Help
 Fast Turtle
 Turn Rays

 Counting
 Scale Distance...
 Turn in Degrees
```

```
Help
 Windows...
 Vocabulary...
 Tools...
 Directions...  ⌘D
 Hints...       ⌘H
.....................
 Options...
```

More on *Geo-Logo's* Linked Windows

The *Geo-Logo* screen looks like this.

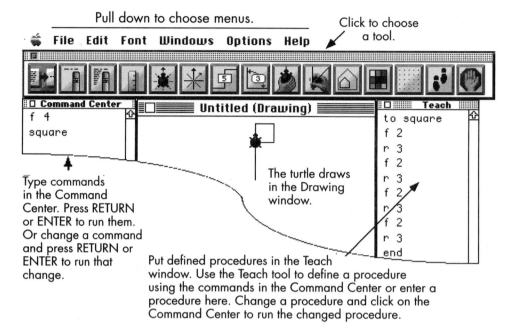

Pull down to choose menus.

Click to choose a tool.

🍎 File Edit Font Windows Options Help

□ Command Center

f 4

square

Type commands in the Command Center. Press RETURN or ENTER to run them. Or change a command and press RETURN or ENTER to run that change.

Untitled (Drawing)

The turtle draws in the Drawing window.

Put defined procedures in the Teach window. Use the Teach tool to define a procedure using the commands in the Command Center or enter a procedure here. Change a procedure and click on the Command Center to run the changed procedure.

Teach

to square
f 2
r 3
f 2
r 3
f 2
r 3
f 2
r 3
end

Command Center

Type commands you wish the turtle to run immediately in the Command Center. Press **<return>** after each command. Make changes to commands directly in the Command Center; they are reflected automatically in the drawing when you press **<return>**. To insert a line, hold down the Command key, then press **<L>**.

Teach Window

When you have a sequence of commands you might wish to use again, you can define them as a procedure. Click on the **Teach tool** . A dialogue box appears, asking for a one-word name for this procedure. The name (with the word *to* in front of it) and the commands (with *end* added) are placed in the Teach window on the right and named as a defined, or taught, procedure. You can then enter the name of the procedure as a new command.

If you change a procedure in the Teach window (for example, changing each f 20 to f 30 in the procedure square above), the change will be reflected in the Drawing window as soon as you click out of the Teach window.

In addition, the **Draw Commands tool** and the **Change Shape tool** , described in Tools on p. 117, allow you to change the geometric figure directly and see the effect on the *symbols* reflected immediately in the Command Center.

This section contains suggestions for how to correct errors, how to get back to what you want to be doing when you are somewhere else in the program, and what to do in some troubling situations.

If you are new to using the computer, you might also ask a computer coordinator or an experienced friend for help.

No *Geo-Logo* Icon to Open

- Check that *Geo-Logo* has been installed on your computer by looking at a listing of the hard disk.
- Open the folder labeled *Geo-Logo* by double-clicking on it.
- Find the icon for the *Geo-Logo* application and double-click on it.

Nothing Happened After Double-Clicking on the *Geo-Logo* Icon

- If you are sure you double-clicked correctly, wait a bit longer. *Geo-Logo* takes a while to open or load and nothing new will appear on the screen for a few seconds.
- On the other hand, you may have double-clicked too slowly, or moved the mouse between your clicks. In that case, try again.

In Wrong Activity

- Choose **Change Activity** from the **File** menu.

Text Written in Wrong Area

- Delete text.
- Click cursor in the desired area or on the desired line and retype text (or select text and use **Cut** and **Paste** from the **Edit** menu to move text to desired area).

Out of Room in Command Center

- Continue to enter commands. Text will scroll, up and old commands will still be there but temporarily out of view. To scroll, click on the up or down arrows in the scroll bar along the right side of the window.

A Window Closed by Mistake

- Choose **Show Window** from the **Windows** menu.

Windows or Tools Dragged to a Different Position by Mistake

- Drag the window back into place by following these steps: Place the pointer arrow in the stripes of the title bar. Press and hold the button as you move the mouse. An outline of the window indicates the new location. Release the button and the window moves to that location.

I Clicked Somewhere and Now *Geo-Logo* Is Gone! What Happened?

You probably clicked in a part of the screen not used by *Geo-Logo*, and the computer therefore took you to another application, such as the "desktop."

- Click on a *Geo-Logo* window, if visible.
- Double-click on the *Geo-Logo* program icon.

The Turtle Disappeared off the Screen. Why?

- If a command moves the turtle off the screen, write the opposite command to make it return. For example, if f20 sent the turtle off the screen, b20 will return it.

   Note: Many versions of Logo "wrap"—that is, when the turtle is sent off the top of the screen, it reappears from the bottom. *Geo-Logo* does not wrap when it is opened because students are learning to connect *Geo-Logo* commands to the geometric figures they draw.

How Do I Select a Section of Text?

In certain situations, you may wish to copy or delete a section or block of text.

- Point and click at one end of the text. Drag the mouse by holding down the mouse button as you move to the other end of the text. Release the mouse button. Use the **Edit** menu to **Copy, Cut,** and **Paste**.

System Error Message

Some difficulty with the *Geo-Logo* program or your computer caused the computer to stop functioning.

- Turn off the computer and repeat the steps to turn it on and start *Geo-Logo* again. Any work that you saved will still be available to open from your disk.

I Tried to Print and Nothing Happened

- Check that the printer is connected and turned on.
- When printers are not functioning properly, a system error may occur causing the computer to "freeze." If there is no response from the keyboard or when moving or clicking with the mouse, you may have to turn off the computer and start over.

I Tried to Print the Drawing Window and Not Everything Printed

- Choose the Color/Grayscale option for printing.
- If your printer has no such option (for example, it may be an older black and white printer), you need to find a different printer to print graphics.

The turtle responds to *Geo-Logo* commands as a robot. If it does not understand a command, or has a suggestion, a dialogue box may appear with one of the following messages. Read the message, click on **[OK]** or press **<return>** from the keyboard, and correct the situation as needed.

Disk or directory full.

> The computer disk is full.

> ■ Use **Save My Work As...** to choose a different disk.

I don't know how to *name*.

> Program does not recognize the *name* command as written.

> | `f50` | needs a space between f and 50 —> f 50 |
> |---|---|
> | `ff50` | extra f |
> | `mypicturje` | misspelling |

I don't know what to do with *name*.

> Either you gave too many inputs to a command, or no command at all.

> | `f 50 30` | needs only one number |
> |---|---|

> You may have left out a command.

> | `5 + 16` | change to `print 5 + 16` |
> |---|---|

I'm having trouble with the disk or drive.

> The disk might be write-protected, there is no disk in the drive, or a similar problem.

> ■ Use **Save My Work As...** to choose a different disk.

***Name* can be used only in a procedure.**

> Certain commands, such as `end` and `stop`, can't be used in the command center.

> ■ Don't use that command if you don't need to.
> ■ Define the procedure in the Teach window.

***Name* does not like *name* as input.**

> A command needs a certain type of input, and didn't get it from the command following it.

> | `f f 30` | Omit one f or put a number after the first one. |
> |---|---|
> | `repeat`
`[f 30 r 90]` | Repeat needs two inputs; a number and a list— for example, `repeat 4 [f 30 r 90]`. |

***Name* is already used.**

A procedure already exists with that name.

- Use a different name.

***Name* needs more inputs.**

Command *name* needs an input, such as a number.

f	needs how much	—> f 30
r	needs how much to turn	—> r 1

Number too big.

There are limits to numbers *Geo-Logo* can use, up to 2147483647.

- Don't exceed the limit.

Out of space.

There is no free memory left in the computer.

- Enter the command `recycle` to clean up and reorganize available memory.
- Eliminate commands or procedures you don't need.
- Save and start new work.

The maximum *value* for *name* is *number*.

The input is too high.

For example, `The maximum value for f is 9999.`

- Use a smaller number.

The minimum *value* for *name* is *number*.

The input is too low a number.

For example, `The minimum value for f is -9999.`

- Use a higher number.

The *Geo-Logo* disk that you received with this unit contains the *Geo-Logo* program and a Read Me file. You may run the program directly from this disk, but it is better to put a copy of the program and the Read Me file on your hard disk and store the original disk for safekeeping. Putting a program on your hard disk is called installing it.

Note: *Geo-Logo* runs on a Macintosh II computer or above, with 4 MB of internal memory (RAM) and Apple System Software 7.0 or later. (*Geo-Logo* can run on a Macintosh with less internal memory, but the system software must be configured to use a minimum of memory.)

To install the contents of the *Geo-Logo* disk on your hard drive, follow the instructions for your type of computer or these steps:

1. Lock the *Geo-Logo* program disk by sliding up the black tab on the back, so the hole is open.

    The *Geo-Logo* disk is your master copy. Locking the disk allows copying while protecting its contents.

    Slide tab→
    up to lock

    Back of disk

2. Insert the *Geo-Logo* disk into the floppy disk drive.

3. Double-click on the icon of the *Geo-Logo* disk to open it.

4. Double-click on the Read Me file to open and read it for any recent changes in how to install or use *Geo-Logo*. Click in the close box after reading.

5. Click on and drag the *Geo-Logo* disk icon (the outline moves) to the hard disk icon until the hard disk icon is highlighted, then release the mouse button.

    The message appears, indicating that the contents of the *Geo-Logo* disk are being copied to the hard disk. The copy is in a folder on the hard disk with the name *Geo-Logo*.

6. Eject the *Geo-Logo* disk by selecting it (click on the icon) and choosing **Put Away** from the **File** menu. Store the disk in a safe place.

7. If the hard disk window is not open on the desktop, open the hard disk by double-clicking on the icon.

    When you open the hard disk, the hard disk window appears, showing you the contents of your hard disk. It might look something like this. Among its contents is the folder labeled *Geo-Logo* holding the contents of the *Geo-Logo* disk.

8. Double-click the *Geo-Logo* folder to select and open it.

   When you open the *Geo-Logo* folder, the window contains the program and the Read Me file.

   To select and run *Geo-Logo*, double-click on the program icon.

Optional

For ease at startup, you might create an alias for the *Geo-Logo* program by following these steps:

1. Select the program icon.

2. Choose **Make Alias** from the **File** menu.

   The alias is connected to the original file that it represents, so that when you open an alias, you are actually opening the original file. This alias can be moved to any location on the desktop.

3. Move the *Geo-Logo* alias out of the window to the desktop space under the hard disk icon.

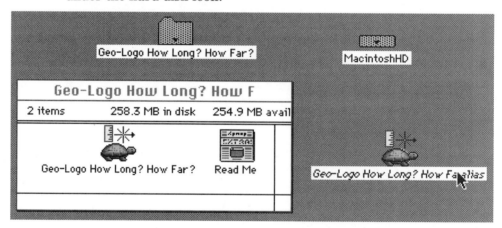

For startup, double-click on the *Geo-Logo* alias instead of opening the *Geo-Logo* folder to start the program inside.

For classroom management purposes, you might want to save student work on a disk other than the program disk. Make sure that the save-to disk has been initialized (see instructions for your computer system).

Saving Work on a Different Disk

☞ 1. Insert the save-to disk into the drive.

☞ 2. Choose **Save My Work As...** from the **File** menu.

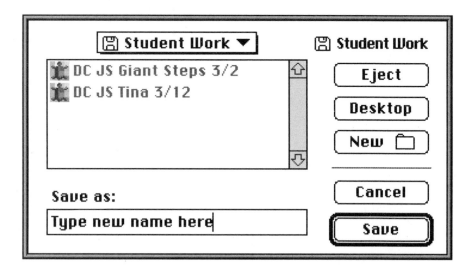

The name of the disk the computer is saving to is displayed in the dialogue box. To choose a different disk, click **[Desktop]** and double-click to choose and open a disk from the new menu.

☞ 3. Type a name for your work if you want to have a new or different name from the one it currently has.

☞ 4. Click on **[Save]**.

As students no longer need previously saved work, you may want to delete their work (called "files") from a disk. This cannot be accomplished from inside the *Geo-Logo* program. However, you can delete files from disks at any time by following directions for how to "Delete a File" for your computer system.

Deleting Copies of Student Work

Blackline Masters

_____ , 19 ____

Dear Family,

Our class is beginning a new math unit called *How Long? How Far?* In this unit, we will be working with important ideas in measurement—measuring the lengths of different objects and finding the lengths of paths.

In the everyday world, we need to know how long things are. We might need to know whether pant legs are long enough, whether a couch will fit along a particular wall, or where to cut lumber to make shelves of equal length. During this unit, your child will find several things in the classroom that are about the same length. Children will use a variety of materials, such as paper strips, craft sticks, and interlocking cubes, as measuring tools to measure and compare length.

Paths are everywhere—roads, sidewalks, trails, and the routes we take to get from one place to another. Often we are interested in the lengths of paths: what's the shortest path or route to work or school? Children will walk to different places in the classroom and the school, describe the paths they took, and compare and measure the lengths of paths. Children will also follow and measure paths using a computer program, *Geo-Logo*.

Here are activities you can try at home:

- Involve your child in measuring activities—hobbies like sewing or carpentry are a natural for this.
- Ask your child to compare the heights or lengths of different objects. For example, is there room for the kitchen table if we move it to the space along that wall?
- Have a measurement scavenger hunt at home. Ask your child to find things that are about as long as different objects. For example, find things that are about as long as one pencil, about as long as two pencils, and about as long as three pencils.
- Compare the heights of family members. Establish a place where heights can be marked off and compared.
- Talk about and compare paths you walk both inside and outside your home. For instance, you might find two paths from the front door to the kitchen. Encourage your child to describe each path as you walk it together. Ask your child to find a way to compare the two paths. Which path is longer?

Happy measuring!

Sincerely,

Weekly Log

Day Box

Monday, _____

Tuesday, _____

Wednesday, _____

Thursday, _____

Friday, _____

Scavenger Hunt 1:
Matching Lengths (A–D)

Find things that are the same length as each paper strip.
Write or draw a picture of what you find.

Strip A	Strip B
Strip C	**Strip D**

Scavenger Hunt 1:
Matching Lengths (E–F)

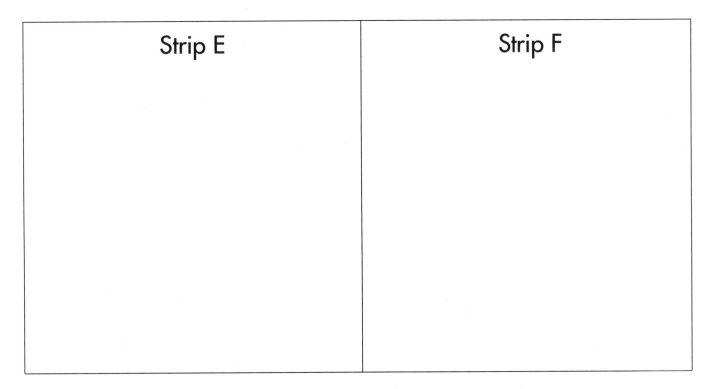

Strip E	Strip F

Write about how you compared objects to the paper strips.
Use words or pictures to show what you did.

© Dale Seymour Publications®

137

Investigation 1 • Session 1
How Long? How Far?

Finding Similar Lengths

Find an object at home or in your neighborhood.
Then find a different object that is about the same
length.

Object 1: _____

Object 2: _____

How did you figure out that the two objects are about
the same length?

_____

_____

_____

_____

_____

_____

© Dale Seymour Publications®

138

Investigation 1 • Session 1
How Long? How Far?

Scavenger Hunt 2:
How Many Paper Strips? (1–4)

Find an object to match each length. Write its name or draw it.

Blue Strips	Yellow Strips
1. Find something 3 blue strips long.	How many yellow strips? Predict _____ Measure _____
2. Find something 2 blue strips long.	How many yellow strips? Predict _____ Measure _____
3. Find something 5 blue strips long.	How many yellow strips? Predict _____ Measure _____
4. Find something 4 blue strips long.	How many yellow strips? Predict _____ Measure _____

© Dale Seymour Publications®

139

Investigation 1 • Sessions 2–4
How Long? How Far?

Scavenger Hunt 2:
How Many Paper Strips? (5–7)

Blue Strips	Yellow Strips
5. Find something 6 blue strips long.	How many yellow strips? Predict _____ Measure _____
6. Find something 7 blue strips long.	How many yellow strips? Predict _____ Measure _____
7. Find something 10 blue strips long.	How many yellow strips? Predict _____ Measure _____

What did you notice?

Measuring Strips

These measuring strips are the same lengths as the blue and yellow strips we used in school. Cut them out and use them for your scavenger hunt at home.

blue
blue
blue

yellow	yellow	yellow	yellow	yellow	yellow

How Far Can You Jump?

Jump three times. Do a frog jump, a rabbit hop, and a kid jump.

a frog jump   a rabbit hop   a kid jump

1. Which jump is the longest? _____

   How many cubes long is it? _____

2. Which jump is the shortest? _____

   How many cubes long is it? _____

3. How many cubes longer is your longest jump than your shortest jump? _____

   Show how you solved the problem.
   Use numbers and words or pictures.

© Dale Seymour Publications®

142

Investigation 1 • Sessions 5–7
How Long? How Far?

Measuring at Home

Use your measuring strips to measure objects at home.

Object: _____

_____ blue strips   _____ yellow strips

Object: _____

_____ blue strips   _____ yellow strips

Object: _____

_____ blue strips   _____ yellow strips

Object: _____

_____ blue strips   _____ yellow strips

Measurement Riddles

Write a measurement riddle for someone at home to solve. You can write about an object you've already measured, or you can choose a new object. Be sure to include 2 or 3 clues and the object's measurements.

_____

_____

_____

_____

_____

_____

Optional

Make up more measurement riddles, or have someone at home make up measurement riddles for you to solve.

_____

_____

_____

_____

A Neighborhood Path

Think of a path you sometimes walk in your neighborhood. Try to picture the path in your mind. Write a description of the path. Include the starting and ending points, any turns you make, and any landmarks you pass.

Starting point: _____

Ending point: _____

A Path in My Neighborhood

_____

_____

_____

_____

_____

_____

_____

© Dale Seymour Publications®

145

Investigation 2 • Session 1
How Long? How Far?

Maze Commands

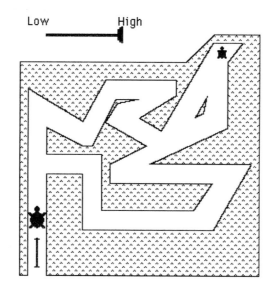

GAME 1

Stepsize _____

_____

_____

_____

_____

_____

_____

_____

_____

Total steps _____

GAME 2

Stepsize _____

_____

_____

_____

_____

_____

_____

_____

_____

Total steps _____

Turtle Turns 1

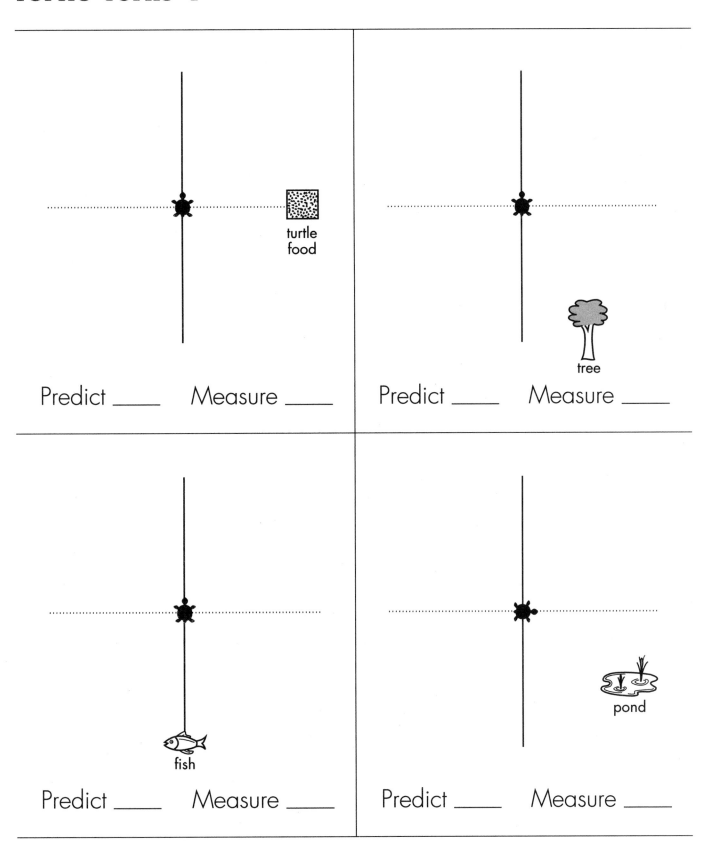

Predict _____ Measure _____

Predict _____ Measure _____

turtle food

tree

fish

pond

Predict _____ Measure _____

Predict _____ Measure _____

Investigation 2 • Sessions 2–3
How Long? How Far?

© Dale Seymour Publications® **147**

Turtle Turns 2

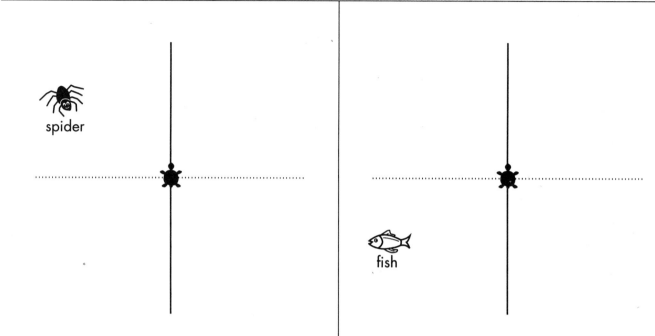

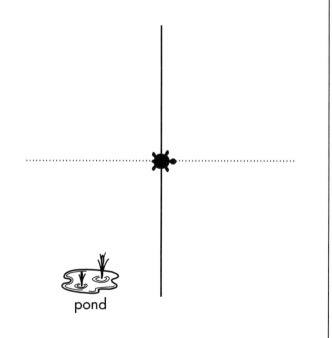

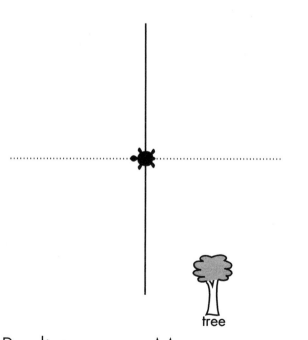

Predict _____ Measure _____

Predict _____ Measure _____

Predict _____ Measure _____

Predict _____ Measure _____

Walking a Path at Home

Think of a path you walk at home, either inside or outside. First, try to imagine it. Then, walk the path. Write a description of it. Include the starting point, the ending point, turns, and landmarks you pass.

Starting point: _____

Ending point: _____

A Path at Home

_____

_____

_____

_____

_____

_____

_____

On the back of this sheet, draw a picture of the path you walked.

© Dale Seymour Publications®

149

Investigation 2 • Sessions 2–3
How Long? How Far?

Today's Number

Make Today's Number, _____,
as many ways as you can using combinations of 10.
For example,

$$23 = \quad + 6 + 5 + 5 + 3$$
$$23 = \quad 10 \quad + \quad 10 \quad + 3$$

Write at least 5 ways here.

_____

_____

_____

_____

_____

© Dale Seymour Publications®

150

Investigation 2 • Sessions 4–5
How Long? How Far?

Andy the Ant Problems

Andy the Ant must walk to school.
He must stay on the sidewalk at all times.

1. Which path from home to school is shortest? (Circle your answer.)

  1 _____

  2 _____

  3 - - - - -

_____

2. How do you know which path is shortest?

  How long is this path?

_____

3. Draw a new path that is the shortest path Andy could walk.
   How long is this path?

_____

4. Draw a new path that is the longest path with only two turns.
   How long is this path?

© Dale Seymour Publications®

151

Investigation 2 • Sessions 6–8
How Long? How Far?

Andy the Ant's Paths

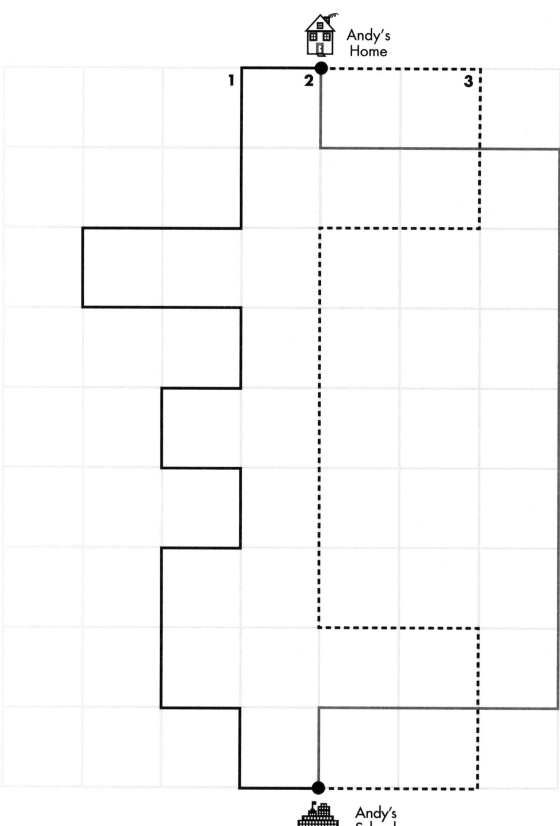

Andy's
Home

1

2

3

Andy's
School

© Dale Seymour Publications®

152

Investigation 2 • Sessions 6–8
How Long? How Far?

Allison the Ant Problems

Allison rides an electric bike around town.
She must stay on the roads at all times.

The bike needs its battery charged every 10 blocks.
The battery can be charged at home or at a charging station.

Charging Station

---

1. Draw a path that will get Allison from
   home, to school, and back home.

   How long is the path?

---

2. Draw a path that will get Allison from
   home, to the library, and back home.

   How long is the path?

© Dale Seymour Publications®

153

Investigation 2 • Sessions 6–8
How Long? How Far?

Allison the Ant's Paths

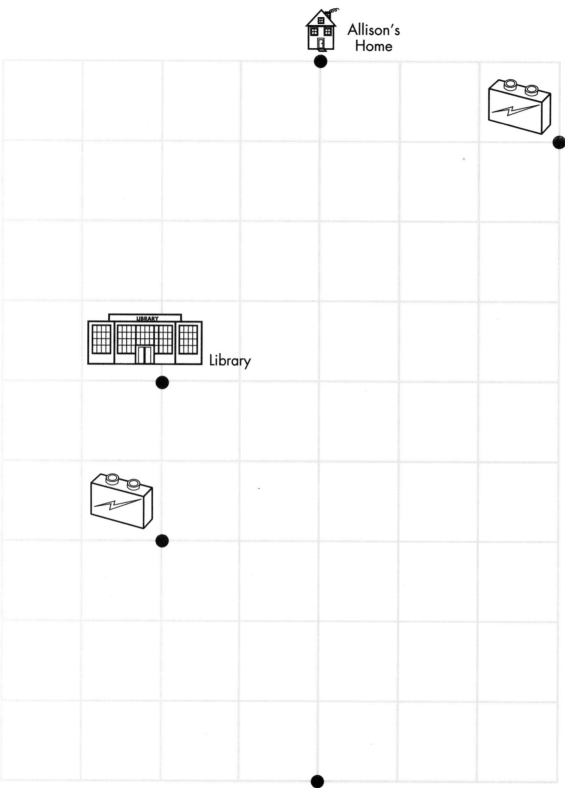

© Dale Seymour Publications® **154**

Investigation 2 • Sessions 6–8
How Long? How Far?

More Allison the Ant Problems

1. Draw a path from Allison's home
   to the library, to school, and back home.

   How long is the path?

---

2. Allison has to go to the post office, library, and school.
   She can go to these places in any order she wants,
   but she must start and end at home.
   Draw a path that she could follow.

   How long is the path?

© Dale Seymour Publications®

155

Investigation 2 • Sessions 6–8
How Long? How Far?

More Allison the Ant's Paths

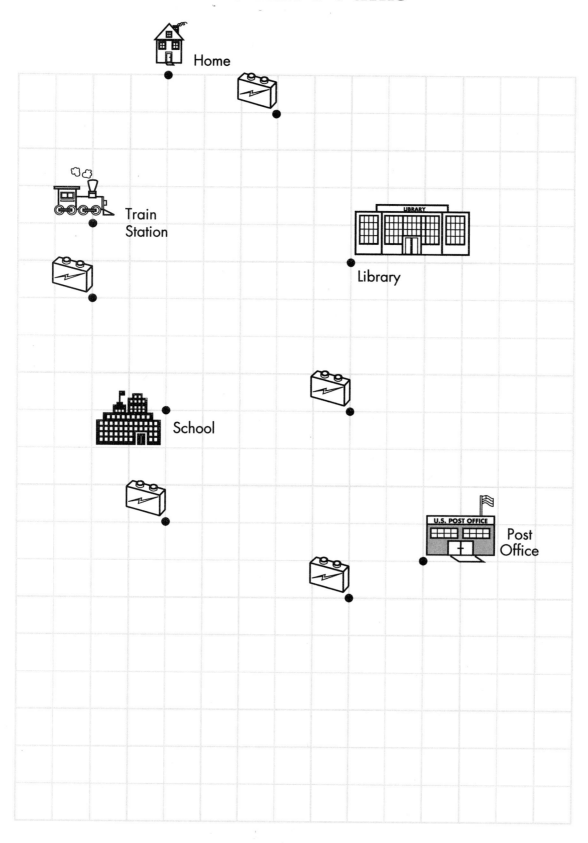

Home

Train Station

Library

School

Post Office

© Dale Seymour Publications® **156**

Investigation 2 • Sessions 6–8
How Long? How Far?

Tina the Turtle Game Commands

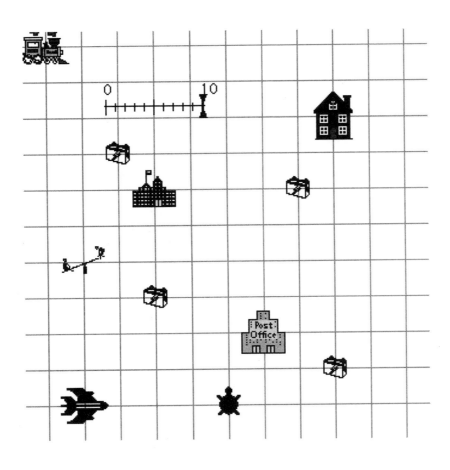

_____

_____

_____

_____

_____

_____

_____

_____

Total distance _____

_____

_____

_____

_____

_____

_____

_____

_____

Total distance _____

© Dale Seymour Publications®

157

Investigation 2 • Sessions 6–8
How Long? How Far?

Three Paths for Andy the Ant

Use three different colors to draw three different paths for Andy the Ant to get to Allison the Ant's home. Remember, Andy always walks on sidewalks.

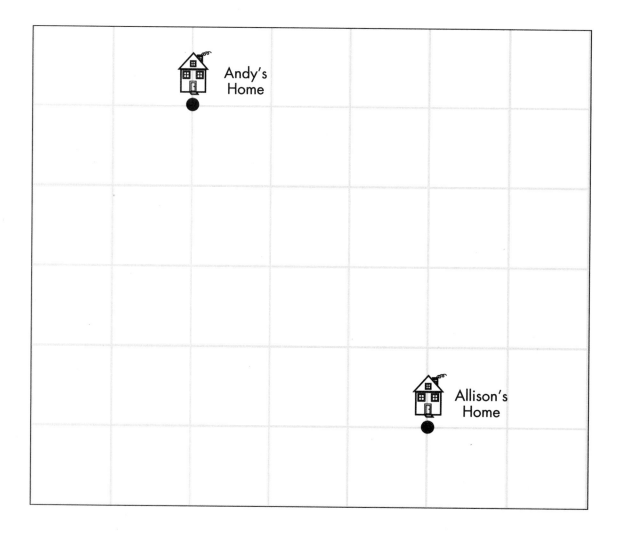

Andy's Home

Allison's Home

How long is each path?

color _____   color _____   color _____

how long? _____   how long? _____   how long? _____

© Dale Seymour Publications®

158

Investigation 2 • Sessions 6–8
How Long? How Far?

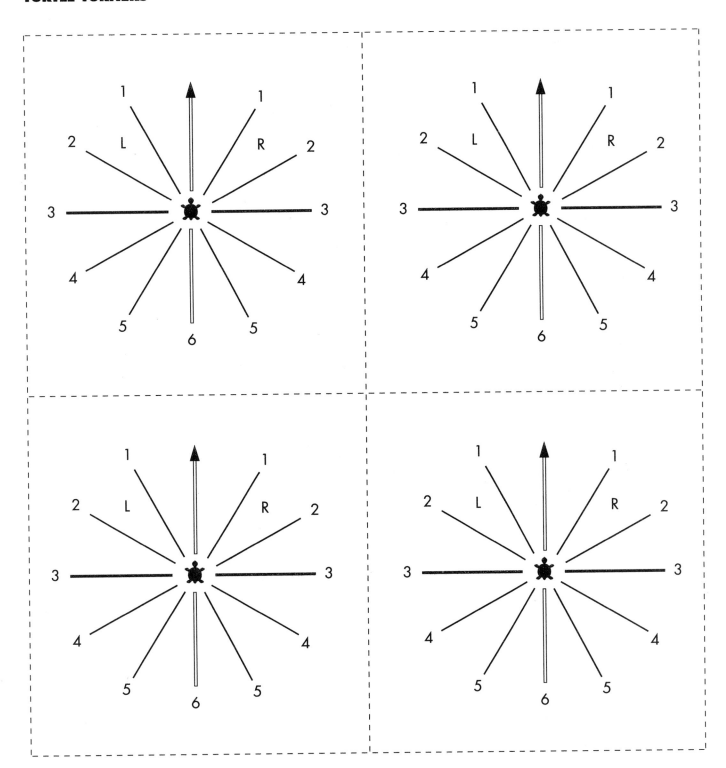

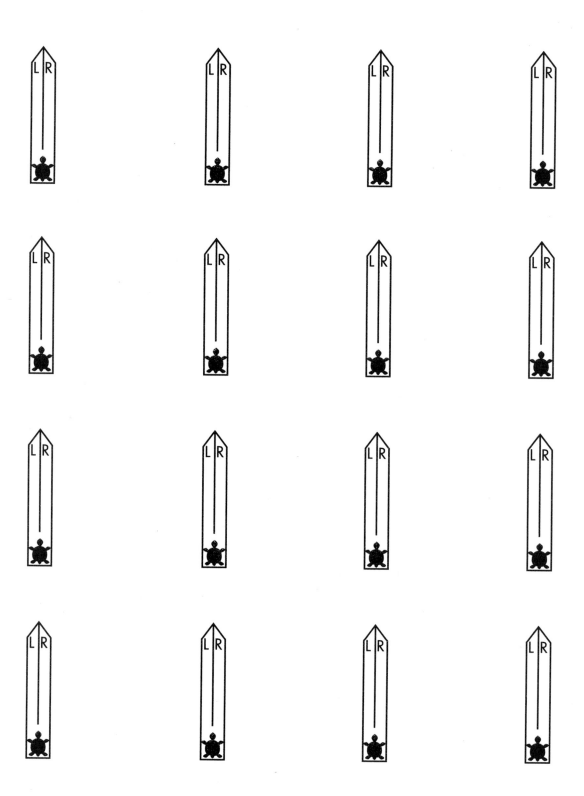

Investigation 2 • Resource
How Long? How Far?

How to Get Started

- ■ Turn on the computer.

- ■ Open *Geo-Logo* with a double-click on the icon.

- ■ Single-click an activity button.

Geo-Logo How Long? How Far?

Geo-Logo Commands

f 5	moves forward 5 turtle steps	**ht**	hides the turtle
b 12	moves back 12 turtle steps	**st**	shows the turtle
l 3	turns left 3 units	**setc red**	sets the color to red
r 2	turns right 2 units		

Tools

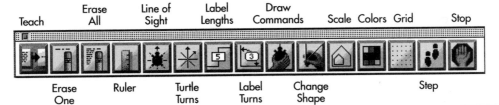

Teach · Erase All · Line of Sight · Label Lengths · Draw Commands · Scale · Colors · Grid · Stop

Erase One · Ruler · Turtle Turns · Label Turns · Change Shape · Step

How to Get Help from *Geo-Logo*

- ■ Choose a topic from the **Help** menu.

How to Open Saved Work

- ■ Turn on the computer, open *Geo-Logo*, select an activity.

- ■ Choose **Open My Work** from the **File** menu.

- ■ Click the name of your work.

- ■ Click **Open**.

How to Save Your Work

- ■ Choose **Save My Work** from the **File** menu.

- ■ First time, type a name like **TM+HS maze 3/23**.

- ■ Click **Save**.

How to Finish

- ■ Finish activity: Choose **Close My Work** from the **File** menu. STOP HERE if changing users.

- ■ Finish *Geo-Logo*: Choose **Quit** from the **File** menu.

- ■ Shut down and turn off the computer.

Practice Pages

This optional section provides homework ideas for teachers who want or need to give more homework than is assigned to accompany the activities in this unit. The problems included here provide additional practice in learning about number relationships and in solving computation and number problems. For number units, you may want to use some of these if your students need more work in these areas or if you want to assign daily homework. For other units, you can use these problems so that students can continue to work on developing number and computation sense while they are focusing on other mathematical content in class. We recommend that you introduce activities in class before assigning related problems for homework.

Turn Over 10   Students play this game in the units *Mathematical Thinking at Grade 2* and *Coins, Coupons, and Combinations*. If your students are familiar with the game, you can simply send home the directions and Number Cards so that students can play at home. If your students have not played the game before, introduce it in class and have students play once or twice before sending it home. You might have students do this activity two times for homework in this unit.

Close to 20   Students are introduced to this game in *Coins, Coupons, and Combinations*. If your students are familiar with the game, you can simply send home the directions, score sheet, and Number Cards so that students can play at home. If your students have not played the game before, introduce it in class and have students play once or twice before sending it home. You might have students do this activity two times for homework in this unit.

Story Problems   Story problems at various levels of difficulty are used throughout the *Investigations* curriculum. The two story problem sheets provided here help students review and maintain skills that have already been taught. You can make up other problems in this format, using numbers and contexts that are appropriate for your students. Students solve the problems and then record their strategies, using numbers, words, or pictures.

Number Strings   This type of problem is introduced in the unit *Coins, Coupons, and Combinations*. Provided here are two sheets of problems. You can also make up other problems in this format, using numbers that are appropriate for your students. For each sheet, students solve the problems and then record their strategies, using words, pictures, or number sentences.

Turn Over 10

Materials: Deck of Number Cards 0–10 (four of each) plus four wild cards

Players: 2 to 3

How to Play

The object of the game is to turn over and collect combinations of cards that total 10.

1. Arrange the cards face down in four rows of five cards. Place the rest of the deck face down in a pile.

2. Take turns. On a turn, turn over one card and then another. A wild card can be made into any number.

   If the total is less than 10, turn over another card.

   If the total is more than 10, your turn is over and the cards are turned face down in the same place.

   If the total is 10, take the cards and replace them with cards from the deck. You get another turn.

3. Place each of your card combinations of 10 in separate piles so they don't get mixed up.

4. The game is over when no more 10's can be made.

5. At the end of the game, make a list of the number combinations for 10 that you made.

Close to 20

Materials: Deck of Number Cards 0–10 (four of each) with the wild cards removed; Close to 20 Score Sheet; counters

Players: 2 to 3

How to Play

The object of the game is to choose three cards that total as close to 20 as possible.

1. Deal five cards to each player.

2. Take turns. Use any three of your cards to make a total that is as close to 20 as possible.

3. Write these numbers and the total on the Close to 20 Score Sheet.

4. Find your score. The score for the round is the difference between the total and 20. For example, if you choose 8 + 7 + 3, your total is 18 and your score for the round is 2.

5. After you record your score, take that many counters.

6. Put the cards you used in a discard pile and deal three new cards to each player. If you run out of cards before the end of the game, shuffle the discard pile and use those cards again.

7. After five rounds, total your score and count your counters. These two numbers should be the same. The player with the lowest score and the fewest counters is the winner.

Close to 20 Score Sheet

PLLAYER 1 — SCORE

Round 1: _____ + _____ + _____ = _____   _____

Round 2: _____ + _____ + _____ = _____   _____

Round 3: _____ + _____ + _____ = _____   _____

Round 4: _____ + _____ + _____ = _____   _____

Round 5: _____ + _____ + _____ = _____   _____

TOTAL SCORE   _____

PLAYER 2 — SCORE

Round 1: _____ + _____ + _____ = _____   _____

Round 2: _____ + _____ + _____ = _____   _____

Round 3: _____ + _____ + _____ = _____   _____

Round 4: _____ + _____ + _____ = _____   _____

Round 5: _____ + _____ + _____ = _____   _____

TOTAL SCORE   _____

0	0	0	0
1	1	1	1
2	2	2	2

3	3	3	3
4	4	4	4
5	5	5	5

6	6	6	6
7	7	7	7
8	8	8	8

Practice Page
How Long? How Far?

9	9	9	9
10	10	10	10
Wild Card	Wild Card	Wild Card	Wild Card

Practice Page A

There are _____ students in our class.

We have 58 plant seeds.
Are there enough for the class? _____
How many leftovers will we have? _____

Explain how you figured this out. You can use numbers, words, or pictures.

Practice Page B

There are _____ students in our class.

We have 44 beans for an activity.
Are there enough for the class? _____
How many leftovers will we have? _____

Explain how you figured this out. You can use numbers, words, or pictures.

Practice Page C

Show how you solved each problem. You can use words, pictures, or number sentences

11 + 2 + 9 =	8 + 17 + 3 =
15 + 3 + 5 =	16 + 2 + 4 + 7 =
12 + 6 + 8 + 5 =	3 + 4 + 15 + 2 =
7 + 2 + 6 + 13 =	3 + 18 + 7 + 12 =

.ctice Page D

Show how you solved each problem. You can use
words, pictures, or number sentences

12 + 3 + 7 =	2 + 14 + 8 =
17 + 5 + 5 + 3 =	6 + 12 + 4 + 8 =
1 + 6 + 8 + 9 + 4 =	2 + 4 + 15 + 4 =
8 + 2 + 4 + 7 + 13 =	2 + 18 + 17 + 13 =